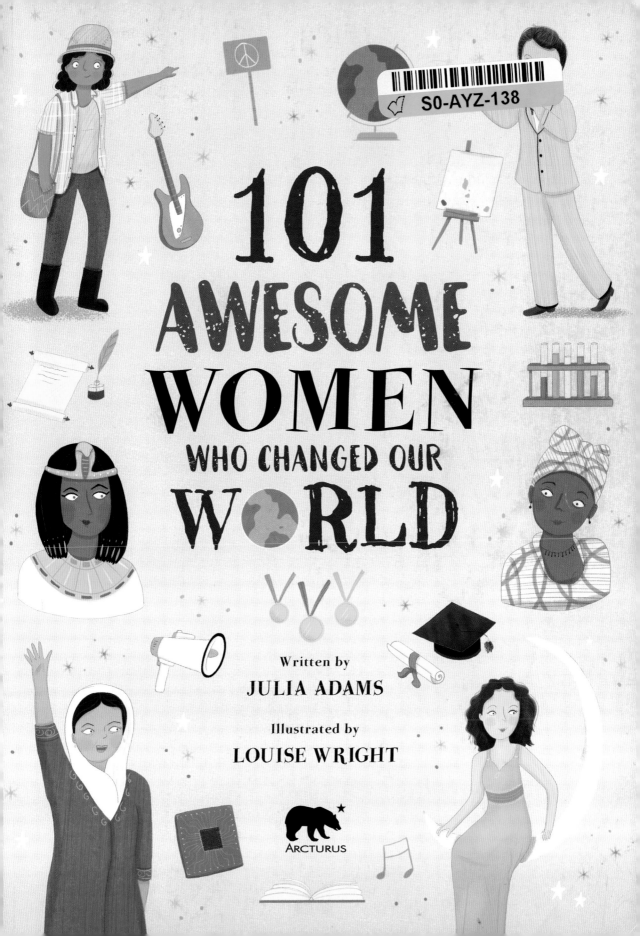

101 AWESOME WOMEN WHO CHANGED OUR WORLD

Written by
JULIA ADAMS

Illustrated by
LOUISE WRIGHT

ARCTURUS

S0-AYZ-138

ARCTURUS

This edition published in 2019 by Arcturus Publishing Limited
26/27 Bickels Yard, 151–153 Bermondsey Street,
London SE1 3HA

Copyright © Arcturus Holdings Limited

All rights reserved. No part of this publication may be reproduced,
stored in a retrieval system, or transmitted, in any form or by any
means, electronic, mechanical, photocopying, recording or otherwise,
without prior written permission in accordance with the provisions of
the Copyright Act 1956 (as amended). Any person or persons who do
any unauthorised act in relation to this publication may be liable to
criminal prosecution and civil claims for damages.

ISBN: 978-1-78888-377-1
CH006248NT
Supplier 26, Date 1118, Print run 8028

Author: Julia Adams
Illustrator: Louise Wright
Designer: Sally Bond
Editor: Susannah Bailey

Printed in China

INTRODUCTION

The course of history is packed with stories of women overcoming odds, defying expectations, and shattering stereotypes. Yet, all too often, their contribution has been overlooked, underplayed, or just forgotten.

Many cultures have believed (or still believe) that women do not need an education, cannot be trusted with leadership, are physically inferior, and are intellectually weak. Men have been privileged, and this means that they have been the world's default decision-makers and history writers.

Jane Goodall
(page 49)

Women, however, have been achieving greatness even when everything seemed against them. The adventurers, scientists, leaders, athletes, and artists in this book are by no means the definitive list of female history-makers, nor are they perfect and without fault, but they are pioneers who stood out, made a difference, and proved without a doubt that they were just as capable as men. Their contributions, both to their field and as an inspiration to others, are worthy of celebration. And that is what this book aims to do.

Arundhati Roy
(page 86)

Sacagawea
(page 114)

CONTENTS

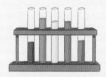

Eva Perón
(page 30)

CHAPTER 1
LEADERS and ACTIVISTS

CHAPTER 2
SCIENTISTS and INVENTORS

Marie Curie
(page 52)

Majlinda
Kelmendi
(page 121)

CHAPTER 3
ARTISTS and WRITERS

CHAPTER 4
ATHLETES and ADVENTURERS

Miriam Makeba
(page 76)

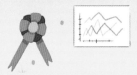

CHAPTER 1

LEADERS
AND
ACTIVISTS

In early cultures, women often had equal status to men—they could be warriors, priestesses, and leaders. But some ancient civilizations, such as Greece and Rome, were founded on different principles. They believed, quite wrongly, that men were natural leaders and that women should stay at home. This harmful point of view persisted for centuries.

Of course, women are just as capable as men and always have been. This chapter introduces strong and clear-sighted queens, politicians, businesswomen, and activists. They have led countries, companies, communities, and campaigns.

As well as doing their job, many of these women have faced and tackled prejudice. Some worked their way up from poor, disadvantaged backgrounds. They all succeeded against the odds.

These activists and politicians were determined to improve the world they lived in. And they were committed to do whatever it took to make changes.

All these women believed in themselves, worked hard to achieve their goals, and never gave up.

Through their efforts and example, they inspired more women to follow their lead. Many of them left the world a safer, fairer place than they found it.

Cleopatra
(*c.*69–30 BCE)

Cleopatra was Egypt's queen when the Roman Empire was at its height. Her deals with Roman leaders Julius Caesar and Mark Antony protected Egypt from invasion. She is one of history's most powerful women.

Boudicca
(*c.*30–*c.*60 CE)

Boudicca was the queen of a Celtic tribe called the Iceni. In 60 CE she led more than 100,000 fellow Celts against the Romans, who had come to capture Britain. The warrior queen had many successes before the Romans defeated her.

Jingu
(*c.*170–*c.*269 CE)

There are countless legends about Empress Jingu of Japan. She is said to have fought alongside the samurai and conquered Korea. She was also believed to be a shaman, who could listen in to the spirit world. In the 1800s, she became the first woman to appear on a Japanese banknote.

BENAZIR BHUTTO
POLITICIAN

(1953–2007)

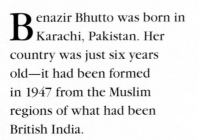
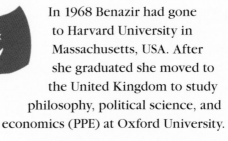

Benazir Bhutto was born in Karachi, Pakistan. Her country was just six years old—it had been formed in 1947 from the Muslim regions of what had been British India.

Benazir's father, Zulfikar Ali Bhutto, was a wealthy politician and landowner. In 1967 he founded the Pakistan People's Party (PPP) and in 1971 he was elected prime minister.

In 1968 Benazir had gone to Harvard University in Massachusetts, USA. After she graduated she moved to the United Kingdom to study philosophy, political science, and economics (PPE) at Oxford University.

In 1977 Benazir returned home to work for her father, who had just been re-elected. However that July the head of the army, General Zia, overthrew the Pakistani government and made himself president. He had Zulfikar executed in 1979, while Benazir and her mother were being held in prison nearby.

After her father's death, Benazir led the PPP and worked with other parties to end military rule. She was imprisoned several times. In 1984 she moved to London, UK. From there she campaigned worldwide for Pakistan's return to democracy.

In 1985 Benazir visited Pakistan to bury her younger brother. She was held under house arrest until she flew back to Europe. The following year she returned for good. Hundreds of thousands of people took to the streets to welcome Benazir home—the crowds were so thick that her motorcade took more than nine hours to drive 12 km (eight miles).

"A people inspired by democracy, human rights, and economic opportunity will turn their back decisively against extremism."

VICTORY GARLAND

In 1988 General Zia called an election. Benazir won and became the first female prime minister of a Muslim country. After just two years in power she was forced to step down because of accusations of illegal activity. In 1993 Benazir was voted back in. Three years later she was removed again. Benazir never served a full, five-year term as prime minister, so she struggled to deliver all she had promised. She built new schools, connected thousands of villages to electricity, and gave the press its freedom. But she had hoped to do much more.

In 1999 there was another military takeover in Pakistan. Benazir lived in exile in Dubai, United Arab Emirates, until democratic elections were reintroduced in 2007. Two bombs went off in the crowd that greeted her return, killing 149 people and injuring 402. Benazir was unharmed, but she was killed two months later by a suicide bomber. Mourners scattered rose petals over her coffin as a sign of their love.

HARRIET TUBMAN
Abolitionist, Army Scout, and Suffragist

(*c.*1820–1913)

"I was the conductor of the Underground Railroad for eight years, and I can say what most conductors can't say—I never ran my train off the track and I never lost a passenger."

Born into slavery in Maryland, USA, Harriet Tubman worked from childhood. Over the years she was a nanny, cook, farmhand, and woodcutter. In 1849 she made the dangerous 145-km (90-mile) journey to Pennsylvania, a free state where slavery was banned. Even here Harriet was not safe. As a runaway slave she could—by law—be captured and returned to her owner.

In 1850 Harriet went back to Maryland to rescue members of her family. She repeated the journey more than 13 times to lead other African-American slaves to freedom. Using a secret route to Canada known as the "Underground Railroad," Harriet rescued more than 70 slaves, putting her own life in great danger.

In the American Civil War (1860–5) Harriet worked as a scout and spy for the Unionists, who wanted slavery abolished. In June 1863 she led Union Army raids on plantations in South Carolina, freeing more than 750 slaves.

Harriet helped others her whole life. She believed that women should be allowed to vote and spoke at suffragist meetings. She gave so much that she died poor— in a care home for elderly African Americans which she had set up.

HELEN KELLER
ACTIVIST AND AUTHOR

(1880–1968)

Helen Keller was born in Alabama, USA. She was a healthy baby, but an illness at the age of 19 months left her deaf and blind. Because she could not hear, Helen did not learn to speak. She became difficult and angry, frustrated by not being understood.

Helen was six years old when her mother found the tutor who would change her life. Partially blind herself, Anne Sullivan recognized that Helen needed discipline, kindness, and—above all—a way to communicate. Anne began by pointing to objects with short, simple names. She used her finger to spell the words into Helen's hand.

"Although the world is full of suffering, it is full also of the overcoming of it."

Helen was a fast learner. Within months she could connect objects with words, read sentences in raised print, and even write with a pen. When she was ten years old, she learned to speak by placing her fingers on her teacher's lips, tongue, and throat and feeling the vibrations.

Helen was the first deaf-blind person to get a college degree. She became an inspirational and world-famous author. Her autobiography *The Story of My Life*, published in 1903, was eventually translated into 50 languages. Helen lectured and campaigned for women's rights, as well as improving conditions for people with disabilities.

HILLARY RODHAM CLINTON
Politician

(b.1947)

Born in Chicago, USA, Hillary Rodham grew up in a household that valued education and hard work. Her parents wanted her to have the same opportunities as her two brothers.

Hillary's interest in politics began while she was still at school. She joined the student council and worked on the school newspaper. When she was taking her degree in political science, Hillary became a supporter of the civil rights movement. She decided to become a lawyer so that she could help to make the system of government fairer.

Hillary studied law at Yale University, Connecticut, and met her future

husband Bill Clinton there. She concentrated on children's rights and family law. After graduating, she eventually moved to Arkansas, where Bill was building a career in the

Democratic Party. The couple married in 1975. Three years later Bill became governor of the state of Arkansas. Hillary continued her law career and was twice named one of the "100 Most Influential Lawyers in America."

In 1992 Bill was elected president. The Clintons moved into the White House in Washington DC with their daughter, who was nearly 12. Hillary didn't want to be the kind of First Lady who stayed

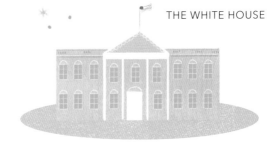

THE WHITE HOUSE

in the background and didn't have a voice. She set up her own office in the West Wing—the part of the White House where the presidential work is done. Hillary hired her own staff and wrote a new health policy, though unfortunately it was never passed.

In 2000 while still First Lady, Hillary was elected as a senator for New York State. She was re-elected at the end of her term of office. Hillary hoped to be the Democrats' presidential candidate in the 2008 election, but when she saw

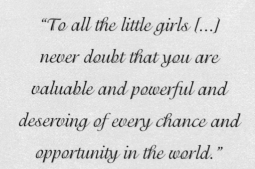

"To all the little girls [...] never doubt that you are valuable and powerful and deserving of every chance and opportunity in the world."

that Barack Obama had more support, she pulled out and backed him instead. Hillary was Secretary of State for President Obama from 2009 until 2013. During that time she visited 112 countries and was a powerful voice for women's and children's rights.

In 2015 Hillary ran for president again and became the first female candidate put forward by a major US party. But in November 2016, in a result that came as a shock to many, Hillary lost the election to Donald Trump.

Not to be defeated, Hillary founded Onward Together in 2017. It funds political groups that share Hillary's vision of a fairer, more inclusive United States.

VOTE HILLARY!

EUFROSINA CRUZ MENDOZA
Human Rights Activist
(b.1979)

Eufrosina Cruz Mendoza was born in a small Zapotec town in the Mexican province of Oaxaca. The Zapotecs are indigenous people with their own language. Women marry young and raise children, but Eufrosina wanted more. She moved away when she was 12 to work and study accounting. She returned when she was 28.

Eufrosina ran for mayor and won, but Oaxaca's laws did not allow women to hold public office or even vote. Eufrosina fought for these basic rights, and as a result the law changed in 2008. She has since founded an organization to support indigenous women and educate them out of poverty. Its symbol is the beautiful, but undervalued, wild arum lily.

FADUMO DAYIB
HUMAN RIGHTS ACTIVIST

(b.1972)

Born in Kenya, East Africa, Fadumo Dayib was deported to her parents' native Somalia in 1989. It was a time of civil war. Fadumo's mother sold all she had to fly her three children to Europe. Fadumo arrived in Finland as an asylum seeker in 1990 with no money and little education. Today she is a health care expert who has worked for the United Nations and studied for a PhD.

In 2016 Fadumo returned to Somalia to run for president—the first woman ever to do so. She lost but has vowed to put pressure on the new government. She wants to bring peace to her country, end corruption, crack down on terrorists, and improve the welfare of women and girls.

DIANE VON FÜRSTENBERG
Fashion Designer and Businesswoman

(b.1946)

Diane Halfin was born in Brussels, Belgium. Her mother was a Holocaust survivor who had been imprisoned at Auschwitz. Diane studied in Spain and Switzerland before moving to Paris and starting her career in the fashion industry. She was married to the German aristocrat Egon von Fürstenberg from 1969 to 1972.

Diane launched her stylish wrap dress in 1974, securing success for her fashion label Diane von Fürstenberg (DVF). Today DVF clothes sell in more than 70 countries, bring in hundreds of thousands of US dollars, and are worn by the rich and famous. In 2010 Diane started the DVF Awards to recognize strong women who transform other women's lives.

SHIRLEY CHISHOLM
POLITICIAN

(1932–2005)

Long before Hillary Clinton or Barack Obama, Shirley Chisholm was breaking down barriers based on sex and race. Born Shirley St. Hill, she was educated in Barbados and New York City, USA. She grew interested in politics while working as a teacher. In 1969 Shirley became the first black woman voted into the US Congress. During her 14 years in the House of Representatives she worked to improve life for women and children, especially in poor areas. In 1972 she was the first black presidential candidate.

Shirley faced prejudice throughout her life. She survived assassination attempts and lived to be 80. Ten years after her death, she was awarded the Presidential Medal of Freedom.

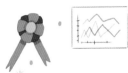

MALALA YOUSAFZAI
EDUCATION ACTIVIST

(b.1997)

Malala Yousafzai was born in Mingora, a city in the Swat Valley in northwestern Pakistan. She was educated in Khushal Public School, which was run by her father Ziauddin.

$$a + b = c$$
$$5 + 3 = 8$$
$$15 + 5 = 20$$
$$4 \times 6 = 24$$

When Malala was ten years old, a group of religious fundamentalists called the Taliban started taking over parts of Pakistan. They outlawed television and music and did not let women leave their homes.

In 2008 the Taliban banned schools in the Swat Valley from teaching girls. Malala's father and many other school leaders bravely refused, even though the Taliban was executing its opponents and blowing up girls' schools.

When Malala was 11, a BBC journalist contacted her father to ask if he knew a schoolgirl who would write about life under the Taliban. Ziauddin suggested Malala. She started her online diary for the BBC in January 2009. To avoid being targeted by the Taliban, Malala used a pseudonym instead of her real name for the blog.

"We realize the importance of our voices only when they are silenced."

Malala's family was proud, but also worried. Ziauddin was a known campaigner for human rights and female education. Sure enough, he received a death threat in May 2009.

Later that year, after the Pakistani army had driven the Taliban out Mingora, Malala was interviewed on television. She spoke openly about the dangers that girls still faced when they went to school because of Taliban groups outside the city.

NOBEL PEACE PRIZE

Malala continued to appear on television and speak out even after her identity as the BBC blogger was made public in December 2009.

In 2011 Malala was nominated for the International Children's Peace Prize and won Pakistan's Youth Peace Prize. But she was receiving death threats. On 9 October 2012 a Taliban gunman shot her in the head.

Two other girls were wounded in the attack. Malala survived but was in a coma for nearly a fortnight. During this time she had hours of surgery to remove the bullet and reduce swelling in her brain. She was flown to the UK for specialist treatment. People around the world followed her story. When Malala eventually recovered, she stayed in the UK to finish her schooling.

In 2013 on her 16th birthday, Malala addressed the United Nations headquarters in New York City,

USA. She demanded that all children have the right to an education. She founded the Malala Fund to raise money to help girls who miss out on education. In 2014, she became the youngest person to be awarded the Nobel Peace Prize.

INDIRA GANDHI
Politician

(1917–84)

Only child Indira Nehru was born into a political family in Allahabad, northern India. Her father Jawaharlal would become the first prime minister of independent India.

> *"My father was a statesman; I am a political woman. My father was a saint; I am not."*

In 1942 Indira married Feroze Gandhi, a journalist and politician. She joined her father's Indian National Congress Party and worked as his assistant. After his death in 1964 she was a government minister. She was elected as India's first female prime minister in 1966 and stayed in power until 1977.

Indira supported the formation of Bangladesh in 1971, worked hard to fight food shortages, and introduced equal pay for women. But in 1975 she was found guilty of election fraud. Instead of resigning, Indira announced a state of emergency. Her decisions over the next two years were often controversial.

Indira lost the 1977 election but won back power in 1980. In 1984 she ordered her army to attack a militant Sikh group that was based in the Golden Temple in

Amritsar. Hundreds of militants were killed, but so were countless innocent worshippers. There was also damage to the temple, which is one of the most sacred Sikh sites in India. Four months after the massacre Indira was assassinated by her Sikh bodyguards.

SHERYL SANDBERG

BUSINESSWOMAN

(b.1969)

Sheryl Sandberg is one of today's most successful and influential business leaders.

Born in Washington DC, USA, Sheryl studied economics at Harvard University, Massachusetts. There she co-founded a group called Women in Economics and Government. One of her tutors was the economist Larry Summers. She later worked for him at the World Bank from 1991 to 1993 and, after completing her masters degree, as his chief of staff at the Treasury Department.

In 2008 Facebook founder Mark Zuckerberg hired Sheryl as his second-in-command. Facebook was four years old and already huge but it wasn't making money. Sheryl brought in advertising and the company was in profit within two years.

In 2013 Sheryl published *Lean In: Women, Work, and the Will to Lead* and launched an online forum called Leanin.org. Both offered inspiration and support to women in business. Her next book, *Option B*, was a response to her husband's sudden death in 2015. It gave advice on recovering from life's difficulties.

In 2001 Sheryl moved into the world of tech when she joined Google. Her job was to find a way for the company to make a profit. She achieved this by selling advertising, and was promoted to vice president.

"A truly equal world would be one where women ran half our countries and companies and men ran half our homes."

SHIRIN EBADI
Human Rights Lawyer and Activist

(b.1947)

Born into an Iranian family that strongly believed in equal rights, Shirin Ebadi grew up knowing that she was worth just as much as her brothers. Her father made sure that Shirin received the same education and opportunities as his sons. This attitude was rare in Iran at the time. Girls were expected to be quiet, obedient, and grow up to run the household.

Shirin attended school and university in Tehran, encouraged by her parents to study law. In 1969 she became Iran's first female judge. She completed her doctorate in law two years later. Shirin was the first woman to be appointed Chief Justice, and was president of the city court of Tehran from 1975 to 1979.

The 1979 Revolution in Iran brought a very strict and traditional Islamic

"Human rights is a universal standard. It is a component of every religion and every civilization."

group to power. Women were stripped of many of their rights. They were no longer allowed to be judges, so Shirin and her female colleagues were demoted to work as clerks. Shirin refused and took early retirement in 1980. For the next 23 years Shirin wrote books and articles about democracy, Islam, and equality for women.

Shirin was finally allowed to work as a lawyer again in 1993. Most of her clients were women, children, and political prisoners and she often worked for free. The Iranian government saw that she was a threat. Shirin faced arrests, a five-year suspended jail sentence, and almost lost her law license. It was only thanks to international pressure that Iran backtracked and allowed her to keep it.

In 2001 Shirin and four other lawyers founded the Defenders of Human Rights Center (DHRC), an organization that raises awareness of human rights issues and supports political prisoners and their families. The DHRC received France's prestigious Human Rights Prize in 2003.

Shirin's tireless work was recognized when she was awarded the Nobel Peace Prize in 2003. She was the first Iranian and the first Muslim woman to receive it.

Shirin supported the One Million Signatures campaign, founded in 2006. Its aim was to collect the signatures of a million Iranians in support of equal rights for women. The government reacted to the pressure by persecuting key members of the campaign and their family members.

In 2009 Shirin publicly announced her distrust of Iran's election results. Not for the first time, her home and offices were raided, some of her possessions were seized, and she received death threats. Shirin went to live in exile in the UK but she has not abandoned her home country. No matter where she is, Shirin will be pushing for human rights in Iran.

ROSA PARKS
CIVIL RIGHTS ACTIVIST

(1913–2005)

7053

In 1955 a simple act of defiance on a local bus led to the birth of the civil rights movement. When Rosa Parks quietly but courageously refused to give up her seat to a white man, she drew attention to the racism she experienced as a black woman in the United States.

Rosa was born Rosa McCauley in Alabama, one of the US states that had segregation laws in place at that time— laws that kept black and white people separate and treated African Americans as second-class citizens. Under these laws, schools for black children were often not as good as white children's schools and it was acceptable to pay black professionals less than white people who were doing the same jobs. Some states even outlawed mixed-race marriage.

Rosa left school when she was 11 years old to look after her sick grandmother. After her grandmother died, Rosa's mother became ill. Rosa ran the household and took care of her mother.

In 1932 Rosa married a barber called Raymond Parks. He encouraged her to return to her studies and in 1933 Rosa completed her high school diploma. Raymond belonged to a civil rights organization called the National Association of the Advancement of Colored People (NAACP). Rosa joined too and became secretary of the Montgomery group.

At the beginning of December 1955, Rosa boarded a bus and

sat in the area where the seats were for black people as usual. After a few stops, some white passengers got on but all the white seats were taken. The bus driver ordered Rosa and a few others to give up their seats. Rosa

refused and was arrested for breaking segregation laws. A few days later, on the day of Rosa's trial, the NAACP organized a boycott of Montgomery's buses. All of the city's 40,000 black workers took part.

That evening the city's black community met and founded the Montgomery Improvement Association (MIA), choosing a Baptist minister called Martin Luther King. Jr, as its leader. The MIA's Montgomery Bus Boycott lasted more than a year. It finally ended in

"I would like to be known as a person who is concerned about freedom and equality and justice and prosperity for all people."

December 1956, when a law was passed to end segregation on buses, trains, and trams. It was an enormous victory for the civil rights movement and the first of many non-violent protests that gradually brought greater equality.

Rosa continued to campaign all her life. She also worked as secretary to the African-American politician John Conyers, another champion of civil rights, for more than 20 years. In 1999 Rosa was awarded the Congressional Gold Medal, one of the highest civilian awards in the United States.

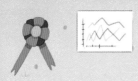

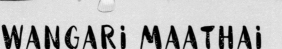

WANGARI MAATHAI
ENVIRONMENTAL ACTIVIST

(1940–2011)

If it weren't for Wangari Maathai, her native Kenya would look radically different. The environmental activist, politician, feminist, human rights campaigner, and scientist improved the situation of hundreds of thousands of Kenyans and other Africans, and also the lands they live in.

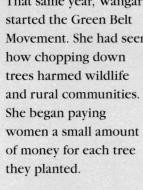

Born Wangari Muta in a village near Mount Kenya, she grew up with breathtaking scenery. Being so close to nature inspired a lot of her later work. After graduating from high school, Wangari studied abroad and in Kenya, earning degrees in biology and a PhD in veterinary anatomy. She taught at Nairobi University and became a professor in 1977.

That same year, Wangari started the Green Belt Movement. She had seen how chopping down trees harmed wildlife and rural communities. She began paying women a small amount of money for each tree they planted.

The movement spread throughout Africa. To date more than fifty million trees have

"We cannot tire or give up. We owe it to the present and future generations of all species to rise up and walk!"

been planted and wildlife is coming back in many areas. The organization has also trained tens of thousands of women so that they can earn a living without harming the environment.

In 2004 Wangari was awarded the Nobel Peace Prize. It recognized the importance of her Green Belt Movement and also her efforts to make Kenya more democratic.

GRAÇA FOSTER
Engineer and Businesswoman

(b.1953)

In Rio de Janeiro, Brazil, the difference between wealth and poverty is stark. While those with money often live in gated communities, the poor inhabit slums called favelas on the outskirts of the city. Housing is makeshift, crime rates are high, and diseases spread fast. Few people escape this poverty, but Graça Foster did just that.

FAVELA HOUSES

Born Maria das Graças, she was raised by her mother in a favela on the edge of Rio. She paid for her school books by collecting trash that could be recycled and selling it. After high school Graça went to university to study chemical engineering.

In 1978 Graça started working for oil giant Petrobras, South America's largest company. In her spare time she studied, completing three more degrees—two in engineering and one in economics. In 1985 she married British-born Colin Foster and took his surname.

Between 2003 and 2005 Graça was an advisor to Dilma Rousseff, the government minister for mines and energy.

Graça returned to Petrobras, joined the board of directors in 2007, and became CEO in 2012. The first woman to head a big oil-and-gas company, Graca was included in *Time Magazine*'s 2012 list of the "100 Most Influential People." Graça left Petrobas in 2015 because of a corruption scandal but she is still respected for reaching the top in a business that is dominated by men.

"I gave up a lot for my career, but I'm very happy for it. I've done what I've always thought was best for me and my family."

BERTA CÁCERES
Human Rights Activist

(1972–2016)

In 2009 a military takeover brought chaos and uncertainty to the Central American country of Honduras. Gang violence increased, there was widespread corruption, and increasing numbers of Hondurans were in extreme poverty. Life was especially hard for women and indigenous peoples. Many thousands fled across the border.

At the same time, the Honduran government radically changed its policies on managing the land. It earmarked huge areas for "megaprojects," such as mines and hydroelectric dams. The people who lived on the land weren't consulted. They were forced to leave and local wildlife was destroyed.

The state did all it could to silence any protests. The activist

"I am a human rights fighter and I will not give up this fight."

Berta Cáceres (born Berta Isabel Cáceres Flores) was especially outspoken. She risked her life to support people's rights and protect the land.

Berta lived in the city of La Esperanza and grew up with a strong sense of social justice. Her mother Austra was an inspirational role model—a midwife, activist, and mayor who took refugee women into her own home.

Berta belonged to the Lenca, the largest indigenous group in Honduras. In 1993 she co-founded the Council of Popular and Indigenous Organizations of Honduras (COPINH). Its aim was to defend Lenca lands, fight logging, dams, and mining projects, and campaign for more health care and schools in Lenca communities.

In 2010 just after the military coup, Lenca people in western Honduras asked Berta and the COPINH to help them stop the Agua Zarca hydroelectric project. The dam was going to alter the course of the Gualcarque river, a source of water and food for many local communities. The locals would have to leave their homes.

Over the next five years, Berta led the campaign to stop the Agua Zarca Dam. She set up human roadblocks to prevent building materials reaching the site. The army and police fired at the protestors on several occasions and Berta received death threats. In 2015 her story was publicized worldwide when she won the Goldman Environmental Prize, which celebrates the work of grassroots environmental activists.

In March 2016 assassins broke into Berta's home and shot her dead. Following Berta's murder, the firms backing the dam pulled out and the project was abandoned. It was a great victory but at a terrible price.

GOLDMAN ENVIRONMENTAL PRIZE 2015

The COPINH marked its 25th anniversary in 2018. In memory of Berta, it continues to take action and coordinate the Lencas' struggle to keep their land.

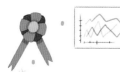

YAA ASANTEWAA
Ashanti Leader

(*c.*1840–1921)

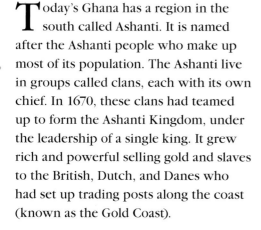

Today's Ghana has a region in the south called Ashanti. It is named after the Ashanti people who make up most of its population. The Ashanti live in groups called clans, each with its own chief. In 1670, these clans had teamed up to form the Ashanti Kingdom, under the leadership of a single king. It grew rich and powerful selling gold and slaves to the British, Dutch, and Danes who had set up trading posts along the coast (known as the Gold Coast).

By the time Yaa Asantewaa was born, the British had taken over the other Europeans' Gold Coast forts. During the 1870s they ransacked the Ashanti capital Kumasi, built a fort opposite the king's palace, and demanded huge taxes.

Yaa Asantewaa was Ashanti royalty. Her brother was chief of Edweso from the 1880s until his death in 1894, when the throne passed to Yaa Asantewaa's grandson Kofi Tene.

"I must say this: if you, the men of Ashanti, will not go forward, then we will. We, the women, will. I shall call upon my fellow women. We will fight!"

In 1896 the British demanded that the Ashanti give up their lands and become part of the British Empire. When King Prempeh I refused, he was captured and deported, along with Kofi Tene and some other chiefs. Yaa Asantewaa took over as chief of Edweso.

GOLDEN STOOL

Even with their king gone, the Ashanti continued to resist British rule. Frustrated, the British governor of the Gold Coast ordered them to hand over the Golden Stool, the most precious and powerful object in the kingdom. It was a sacred symbol, kept in a secret place known only to the king and his trusted officials.

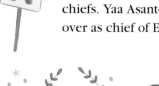

The Ashanti chiefs met to discuss the humiliating demand. The Golden Stool was the foundation of their society—handing it over would spell the end of Ashanti independence. Yaa Asantewaa was the guardian of the Golden Stool at the time. Seeing the fear all around her, she fired a gun into the air and rallied the chiefs with a rousing speech.

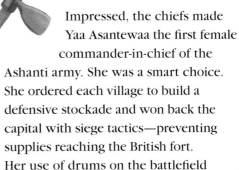

Impressed, the chiefs made Yaa Asantewaa the first female commander-in-chief of the Ashanti army. She was a smart choice. She ordered each village to build a defensive stockade and won back the capital with siege tactics—preventing supplies reaching the British fort. Her use of drums on the battlefield

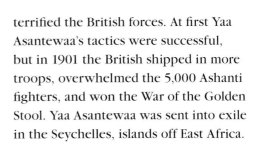

terrified the British forces. At first Yaa Asantewaa's tactics were successful, but in 1901 the British shipped in more troops, overwhelmed the 5,000 Ashanti fighters, and won the War of the Golden Stool. Yaa Asantewaa was sent into exile in the Seychelles, islands off East Africa.

The Gold Coast region was under British rule, but the Ashanti king and chiefs were eventually allowed to return. Yaa Asantewaa's bravery was celebrated in songs and, in 1957, Ghana gained independence once more.

EVA PERÓN
FIRST LADY OF ARGENTINA

(1919–52)

Eva Perón (born Eva Maria Duarte) became an important political figure in Argentina without ever being elected. She grew up in extreme poverty, but became a successful film and radio actor.

In 1945 Eva married politician Juan Perón. When he became president, "Evita" (as the people called her) unofficially ran two government departments. She increased wages and funded hospitals, orphanages, schools, and care homes. She also helped to pass the law that gave women the right to vote. In 1951 Eva's followers begged her to stand for vice president, but she was ill with cancer. She died aged 33, but remains an icon to this day. Her story is the subject of a popular musical, *Evita* (1976).

INDRA NOOYI
Businesswoman

(b.1955)

Indra Nooyi (born Indra Krishnamurthy) studied physics, chemistry, and mathematics at the university in her home town of Madras (now Chennai) in southern India. In 1978 she moved to the United States to complete a two-year masters degree at Yale in Connecticut.

Indra was a business consultant before joining PepsiCo, the world's second-largest food and drink company. By 2006 she was its first female CEO. Within ten years Indra had boosted PepsiCo's profits by 160 percent. She also responded to changing lifestyles by introducing healthier products. Indra values her staff. Each year she writes a personal letter to each of her 400 senior executives' parents, thanking them for their child's valuable contribution.

LEYMAH GBOWEE
PEACE ACTIVIST

(b.1972)

Leymah Gbowee was born in Liberia, West Africa. When she was 17 years old civil war broke out and she fled to Ghana as a refugee. She trained as a social worker and counsellor so she could help traumatized child soldiers.

In 2000 Leymah was at the first Women in Peacebuilding Network (WIPNET) meeting. In 2002 she organized Liberian women from all religious backgrounds to hold peaceful protests against the civil war. Eventually their pressure resulted in peace talks and the 14-year war ended. In 2009, Leymar won the Nobel Peace Prize. Today she runs the Gbowee Peace Foundation Africa which educates girls, teenagers, and women in West Africa.

ANGELA MERKEL
Politician

(b.1954)

BRANDENBURG GATE, BERLIN

When Angela Merkel (born Angela Dorothea Kasner) came into the world, Germany was split into two states: West Germany and the German Democratic Republic (GDR). Angela was just a baby when her parents moved from Hamburg, West Germany, to the GDR. She grew up and was educated there.

Just after the Berlin Wall came down in 1989, Angela joined the Christian Democratic Union (CDU). She wanted to shape the new, unified Germany. In 2000 she took over as CDU leader and in 2005 she became the first female German chancellor (head of government). Multiple re-elections made Angela the longest-serving head of state in the European Union (EU). Hillary Clinton has described her as "the most important leader in the free world."

EMMELINE PANKHURST

WOMEN'S RIGHTS ACTIVIST

(1858–1928)

Emmeline Pankhust (born Emmeline Goulden) grew up in Manchester, UK, in a politically active family. Democracy and suffrage (the right to vote) were the big issues of the day. Only five percent of Britain's population had the vote at that time—they were men who owned property above a certain value.

In 1897 Emmeline married Richard Pankhurst, a lawyer who believed in women's suffrage. He wrote two acts of parliament to ensure women could keep their earnings and property instead of giving it to their husbands.

In 1889 Emmeline founded the Women's Franchise League. Five years later it won the right of married women to vote in local elections.

BALLOT BOX

In 1903 Emmeline started the Women's Social and Political Union (WSPU), with the aim of securing full, equal voting rights for women. The WSPU's motto was "Deeds not Words" and it adopted fierce and often violent tactics to draw attention to its cause.

WSPU members, who became known as "suffragettes," demonstrated on the streets, smashed windows, and started fires. If they were imprisoned, they went on hunger strike. The authorities feared public outcry if the women died of starvation and resorted to force-feeding, a horrible and dangerous procedure. From 1913 the so-called Cat and Mouse Act allowed prisons to release hunger strikers long enough to regain their health, then rearrest them. Suffragette Emily Davison went on seven hunger strikes and was force-fed 49 times. She died in June 1913 by walking out in front of the king's horse during a race at the Epsom Derby.

Emmeline and her daughters Christabel and Sylvia were behind many of the suffragettes' activities. In 1913, Emmeline went on a lecture tour of the United States to raise funds. She looked frail but was mentally strong. In the previous 18 months she had gone to prison 12 times and spent 30 days behind bars, all on hunger strike.

When World War I (1914–18) broke out, Emmeline stopped all WSPU activities.

VOTES FOR WOMEN

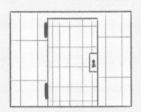

"We are here not because we are lawbreakers; we are here in our efforts to become lawmakers."

The government freed imprisoned suffragettes so they could help with the war effort. Once the war was over the government granted women over 30 the right to vote—but by then all men over 21 could vote. Emmeline continued her campaign, giving talks across the United States, Canada, and Russia.

In 1927 back in the United Kingdom, Emmeline was chosen to stand for parliament, but she was not in good health. She died in June 1928, just weeks before a law was passed which finally gave women the same voting rights as men.

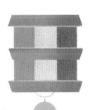

RIGOBERTA MENCHÚ
HUMAN RIGHTS ACTIVIST

(b.1959)

When she wasn't at school, Rigoberta Menchú spent her childhood helping out in the fields. Her family struggled to survive and often had to travel to the coast to work on coffee plantations.

Rigoberta is one of the Maya, indigenous people of Mexico, Guatemala, and Belize. Her group, the K'iche' people, live in the highlands of Guatemala. Rigoberta's father was an activist and she joined him on visits to nearby communities to teach people their rights. It was dangerous but important work. Guatemala was in the grip of a civil war that had begun in 1960. The army and security forces were constantly threatening people or making them "disappear."

In the 1970s many Maya, including Rigoberta and her family, started to protest. They wanted to end injustice, have a say in how their country was run, and be recognized as full citizens. People from Mayan communities were extremely poor and had no basic rights.

The authorities responded to the demonstrations and rallies with a sustained and violent offensive. In 1979 soldiers kidnapped, tortured, and killed Rigoberta's mother and brother. Her father died the following year when police set fire to the Spanish embassy in Guatemala City, which was being occupied by K'iche' protestors. Over the next few years more than 200,000 indigenous people lost their lives.

In 1996 the 36-year Guatemalan Civil War finally ended. Rigoberta became a UNESCO Goodwill Ambassador with special responsibility for indigenous peoples.

Rigoberta realized that trials for war crimes such as torture or genocide might be corrupt if they take place in Guatemala. She has urged Spain to demand the handover of criminals and has had some success.

Rigoberta went to live in exile in Mexico. She wrote her autobiography *I, Rigoberta*, which was published in 1983. It brought the suffering of the Maya to the rest of the world's attention.

In 1992 Rigoberta was awarded the Nobel Peace Prize for her work defending the rights of indigenous peoples and trying to find a peaceful end to the civil war. She used the prize money to found the Rigoberta Menchú Tum Foundation, which aims to improve indigenous lives through education and political engagement.

Rigoberta ran for president in 2007 and 2011. Meanwhile her foundation continues to seek justice for Mayan survivors of the war. It has also replaced the all-colonial history taught in university with a multicultural story that has meaning for all Guatemalans. Rigoberta is president of *Salud para Todos* (Health for All), which aims to supply indigenous people with low-cost medicines.

"What I treasure most in life is being able to dream. During my most difficult moments and complex situations I have been able to dream of a more beautiful future."

CHAPTER 2

SCIENTISTS AND INVENTORS

From biochemists and physicists to volcanologists, mathematicians, and engineers, women have been shaping the worlds of scientific research and invention for centuries.

Even though they had fewer opportunities than men, many female scientists and inventors have reached the top of their fields. Some had to leave their home countries—either to escape political persecution or to access schooling, research money, or jobs—and many were not given recognition for their achievements. All of them had to deal with the mistaken and damaging idea that men were more gifted than women at science and technology.

In this chapter, we meet some of the incredible women who refused to accept outdated, sexist notions and were willing to tackle prejudice head-on. Their achievements include numerous scientific breakthroughs and discoveries, as well as the invention of technologies that were far ahead of their time.

Maria Sibylla Merian

(1647–1717)

Maria Sibylla Merian was a German naturalist and scientific illustrator who specialized in entomology. She made detailed paintings of the life cycles of nearly 200 insects and her work was the first proper investigation into the process of metamorphosis (transformation).

Françoise Barré-Sinoussi

(b.1947)

In 1983 the French virologist Françoise Barré-Sinoussi was part of the team that discovered HIV, the virus that causes AIDS. Thanks to her work, treatment for AIDS sufferers has improved dramatically. Françoise was awarded the Nobel Prize for her work in 2008.

Working to the very best of their abilities, these women have shone in their chosen areas. They didn't always receive the same recognition as their male equals, but their monumental contributions to science and technology have helped to improve the lives of us all and to move humankind forward.

MAMIE PHIPPS CLARK
SOCIAL PSYCHOLOGIST

(1917–83)

Mamie Phipps was born into a divided, unfair society. There was racial segregation across the United States, but especially in southern states such as Arkansas, where Mamie grew up. African Americans had separate schools, hospitals, and prisons, and they had their own entrances to cinemas and sports grounds. They were not even allowed to sit on certain bus seats or park benches. The education in schools for African-American children was often poorer than in "white" schools.

Despite these disadvantages, Mamie worked hard, completed school, and won a university scholarship. She began a degree in mathematics and physics, but soon switched to psychology. In her final year she married Kenneth Bancroft Clark, who was studying to be a doctor of psychology. After graduating, Mamie began a master's degree. She researched how African-American

children in segregated communities saw themselves—a field of study that nobody had ever looked at before.

Mamie and Kenneth were the first African Americans to graduate as doctors from Columbia University, New York City. In the 1940s they carried out "doll tests" that built on Mamie's original research. The Clarks interviewed young African-American children from segregated and non-segregated areas. They showed the children dolls that were identical, apart from being either white with yellow hair or

black with brown hair. They asked the children if they felt that they looked more like one doll than the other. They also asked the children if they liked one of the dolls more, and if so, why.

The results of the study were shocking. Most of the children—especially those from segregated areas—preferred the white doll. They thought the black one was ugly and bad, but they also believed that they looked like the black doll. Mamie and Kenneth saw that segregation had damaged the black children's self-esteem and made them think they were not as good as the white children. Something had to change. They needed to be treated as equals.

In 1954 the court case *Brown vs. Board of Education* used the Clarks' study as proof that segregation was harming black children. As a result, school segregation was banned in the United States.

"I think that whites and blacks should be taught to respect their fellow human beings as an integral part of being educated."

Mamie faced prejudice as an African-American woman, but she finally found a fulfilling job when she opened the Northside Center for Child Development in 1946. It provided support for children who had emotional problems. Mamie improved the lives of countless young people from poor and minority backgrounds.

RITA LEVI-MONTALCINI
NEUROBIOLOGIST

(1909–2012)

Although her father thought that a woman's duty was to be a wife and mother, Rita Levi-Montalcini had her own ideas. Determined to be a doctor, she graduated from the medical school in Turin, Italy, in 1936. Her plans to spend three more years studying the human brain were blocked—not because she was a woman, but because of her Jewish faith. Italy's leader Benito Mussolini was an ally of Germany's Adolf Hitler. To show his support for Hitler, Mussolini introduced race laws that made Jews second-class citizens.

"Above all, don't fear difficult moments. The best comes from them."

With Jews forbidden to work as doctors or carry out academic research, Rita set up a secret lab at her parents' house. She studied chicken embryos' nerve cells with homemade instruments. She had to move house once, taking all her equipment with her. Despite the difficulties, Rita made ground-breaking discoveries that would explain how cancer spreads.

NERVE CELL

In 1946 Rita took a position at the university in St Louis, USA. She repeated the chicken embryo experiments with biochemist Stanley Cohen. The pair discovered the protein that controls nerve growth and were joint winners of the Nobel Prize in 1986.

Rita was also awarded membership of the European Molecular Biology Organization (EMBO) and made a senator for life in the Italian government. She worked right up to her death, aged 103.

NETTIE STEVENS
Geneticist

(1861–1912)

Born in Vermont, USA, Nettie Stevens grew up in an era when it was unusual for girls to be educated. Luckily for her, she was able to attend a school that welcomed girls. Nettie had to work as a teacher and librarian to save up enough money to go to college and was 39 by the time she left Stanford, California, with her masters degree.

Nettie took a research position at Bryn Mawr, a women-only college in Pennsylvania. She studied mealworms and other insects to work out what decides an offspring's sex. Nettie showed that chromosomes (lengths of DNA) come in pairs—females have two X chromosomes (XX), while males have an X and a Y (XY). Offspring always receive one X chromosome from their mother, but can receive an X or a Y from the father. If it's a Y, the offspring will be male. X chromosomes had been identified in 1900, and Nettie named her discovery the Y chromosome because it follows X in the alphabet.

It took time before scientists accepted the idea that chromosomes determine sex. Nettie's research career was only short—sadly, she died aged 50—but in that time she made great leaps that helped us to understand genes.

> "Her single-mindedness and devotion, combined with keen powers of observation; her thoughtfulness and patience, united to a well-balanced judgement, account, in part, for her remarkable accomplishment."

NOBEL LAUREATE THOMAS HUNT MORGAN ON NETTIE STEVENS

ADA LOVELACE
Mathematician

(1815–52)

Ada King, Countess of Lovelace was born in London (then Middlesex), UK. Her parents—the famous poet Lord Byron and mathematician Annabella Milbanke Byron—separated five weeks after Ada's birth, so she never got to know her father.

Determined to give Ada a good education, Annabella hired private tutors. Most of Ada's schooling was in science, logic, and mathematics. Annabella believed that studying would keep Ada out of trouble. She was worried that Ada might have inherited her father's wildness— Lord Byron was always being involved in scandals, and Ada's mother didn't want Ada to follow in his footsteps.

Ada met Charles Babbage at a party when she was 18. Charles was an inventor who became famous for his work on the earliest forms of computers. He showed Ada the prototype of a mechanical calculator called the Difference Engine. He also talked to her about a complex computing machine that he had just started to design. Called the Analytical Engine, it would be

> "That brain of mine is something more than merely mortal, as time will show."

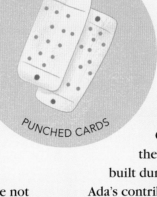

PUNCHED CARDS

programmed using punched cards. Ada was fascinated by the machine's possibilities.

Ada married at 20 and started a family but her mathematical studies were not interrupted for long. In 1842 the Italian mathematician Luigi Menabrea asked Ada to translate an article he had written about the Analytical Engine, recognizing that she had the language skills and mathematical understanding to do a great job.

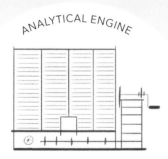

ANALYTICAL ENGINE

Ada not only translated the article, but she also added her own detailed annotations and explanations. When the article was published in 1843, Ada was praised for its insightful, comprehensive notes. She clearly had a unique grasp of Charles Babbage's vision. Charles himself was in awe of her mathematical

talent and ability to formulate complex calculations.

Only a small section of the Analytical Engine was built during Charles' lifetime, but Ada's contributions are valued to this day. Her instructions to make the Analytical Engine solve problems are now considered the "first programming language." A century later, in the 1940s, the English computer scientist Alan Turing referred to Ada's notes while developing some of the first modern computers.

Ada died of cancer when she was just 36 years old, but her name lives on. Every year, on the second Tuesday in October, people around the world mark Ada Lovelace Day. It celebrates the achievements of women in science, technology, engineering, and mathematics (STEM).

LISE MEITNER
Physicist

(1878–1968)

Lise Meitner grew up in Vienna, Austria, at a time when girls could not go to school after the age of 14. However, as soon as Austrian universities started accepting women, she sat the entrance exam and was accepted. Lise went on to become one of the very first women in the world to hold a PhD in physics.

NUCLEAR FISSION

Lise discovered nuclear fission, the process that powers the atomic bomb. To her lifelong disappointment, the Nobel Prize for its discovery was unfairly awarded solely to her fellow (male) scientist Otto Hahn. However, Lise did win many other awards and even has a radioactive element, meitnerium, named after her.

ELIZABETH BLACKBURN
BIOCHEMIST

(b.1948)

Born on the island of Tasmania, Australia, Elizabeth Blackburn studied biochemistry at Melbourne University and was awarded her PhD from Cambridge, UK. In the early 1980s, she discovered telomerase. The protective tips on the end of chromosomes are called telemeres, and over time they shorten and are unable to protect the chromosomes. Telomerase slows down this shortening. Elizabeth and her colleagues Carol Greider and Jack Szostak won a Nobel Prize for their work.

In 2017 Elizabeth co-wrote a book about living longer to show that genes are only part of the story. Eating healthily, exercising, and using techniques such as mindfulness to reduce stress can stop cell decay and slow down aging.

MAY-BRITT MOSER
Psychologist and Neuroscientist

(b.1963)

May-Britt grew up on a remote farm in Fosnavåg, Norway, then moved to Oslo to study psychology and neurobiology. During this time she met Edvard Moser and they married in 1985. The Mosers worked together on spatial awareness—how the brain allows us to understand where we are at any given moment. They discovered the neurons (nerve cells) that look after spatial awareness and some memory in the hippocampus, a small organ deep in the brain.

In 2014 May-Britt and Edvard were awarded the Nobel Prize for Physiology or Medicine, along with their mentor, American-British neuroscientist John O'Keefe. Their discovery has helped us to understand more about human memory and brain diseases such as Alzheimer's.

KATIA KRAFFT
VOLCANOLOGIST

(1942–91)

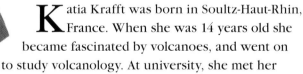

Katia Krafft was born in Soultz-Haut-Rhin, France. When she was 14 years old she became fascinated by volcanoes, and went on to study volcanology. At university, she met her future husband Maurice Krafft. The two shared a fearless passion for volcanoes and became the first scientists to study, film, and photograph eruptions and lava flows up close.

Katia and Maurice used their knowledge to educate communities close to volcanoes on how to stay safe. Their work, along with their predictions of volcanic eruptions, have helped to save millions of lives worldwide. Tragically, Katia and her husband were killed during the eruption of a volcano in Japan in 1991.

MARYAM MIRZAKHANI
MATHEMATICIAN

(1977–2017)

In July 2017 most Iranian newspapers made an unthinkable decision— they broke the dress code of only showing women wearing the hijab (traditional veil) and featured a woman with uncovered hair. Their front pages paid tribute to a national hero, the mathematician Maryam Mirzakhani, who had died of cancer aged 40.

Maryam was born in Tehran and her childhood was overshadowed by war. In 1979 the Islamic leader Ayatollah Khomeini led the Iranian Revolution, overthrowing the shah (king) and founding an Islamic republic. Then came the Iran-Iraq War (1980-88), which brought hardship and huge changes to how the country was run. Later, Maryam insisted she was lucky— had she been a teenager during the war, she would have had far fewer educational opportunities.

Maryam attended a school for gifted and talented girls. At first she had no interest in mathematics and her ambition was to become a writer. Toward the end of her school years, her brother introduced her to complicated mathematical problems and their solutions. Maryam was fascinated and wanted to learn more. She obviously had a flair for mathematics and, most importantly, she really enjoyed it, too.

In 1994 Maryam became the first girl to represent Iran at the International Mathematical Olympiad, winning a gold for her country. She repeated this feat in 1995. She went on to study mathematics at Sharif University, Iran's top science institution. After graduating in 1999, Maryam emigrated to the United States. She was awarded a PhD at Harvard University in 2004.

Maryam specialized in the intricate mathematics of curved surfaces. She developed formulas for finding the surface areas of increasingly complicated rounded, irregular shapes.

Although Maryam was working with incredibly difficult, abstract ideas, she took a refreshingly playful and visual

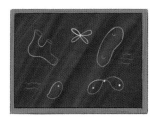

approach. She often drew shapes and doodles on blackboards or pieces of paper, scribbling equations all around them. This process helped Maryam to think and move forward. She had an unusually gifted and creative mind for problem solving.

"The beauty of mathematics only shows itself to more patient followers."

In 2014 Maryam became the first woman to be awarded the Fields Medal. Given every 4 years, this is an exceptional prize for mathematicians and is similar in importance to the Nobel Prize.

Maryam's mathematical contribution has been useful in many fields. In cosmology, her formulas have enabled physicists to explore the curved nature of the Universe. They have also furthered research and design in engineering, materials, and even computer encryption (turning information into a scrambled code).

ROSALIND FRANKLIN
Chemist and X-Ray Crystallographer

(1920–58)

Born in London, UK, Rosalind Franklin knew by the age of 15 that she wanted to be a scientist. She studied natural sciences at Newnham, one of only two Cambridge University colleges that admitted women at that time. In 1945 Rosalind left Cambridge with a PhD in physical chemistry.

Rosalind went to work at King's College, London in 1951, after a spell in Paris learning X-ray crystallography—taking X-ray images of the atoms or molecules

"Science and everyday life cannot and should not be separated."

that make up crystals. Rosalind used the technique to "photograph" DNA, the molecule that stores our genes (instructions for life).

Photo 51, Rosalind's detailed X-ray image of DNA, helped the molecular biologists Francis Crick, James Watson, and Maurice Wilkins identify the structure of DNA as a twisted-ladder shape, or double helix. They used Photo 51 without

PHOTO 51

Rosalind's permission, and without crediting her. In 1962 the three men won a Nobel Prize in Chemistry.

Knowing the structure of DNA has enabled us to develop new medicines, understand illnesses better, and even grow stronger crops. Today we know how important Rosalind's work was. Prizes, grants, laboratories, computer software, and even an asteroid have been named after her.

JANE GOODALL

Primatologist, Ethologist, and Anthropologist

(b.1934)

Born Valerie Jane Morris-Goodall in London, UK, Jane loved animals from an early age. Her dream was to travel to Africa to study apes.

same time day after day. Eventually her patience paid off.

Jane established a unique and close relationship with the chimpanzees and was able to make groundbreaking discoveries. She reported that they had complex social lives, showed emotions such as empathy, and even used tools. Until then scientists thought that only humans used tools.

In the 1980s, when the chimpanzees' habitat became endangered, Jane started campaigning to protect the apes. She has founded conservation organizations and written books that have changed the way we see ourselves as humans, as well as how we view animals. Since 2002, Jane has also served as a United Nations Messenger of Peace.

In 1957 Jane went to work as a secretary in Kenya. She met Louis Leakey, the archaeologist and paleontologist who had discovered early hominids (human ancestors). Louis set up a long-term project for Jane to study chimpanzees in their habitat in Tanzania.

Armed with binoculars and a notepad, Jane set to work. At first the chimpanzees didn't trust her, but Jane continued to visit the same spot at the

"Only if we understand, will we care. Only if we care, will we help. Only if we help, shall all be saved."

MARY ANNING
Paleontologist

(1799–1847)

To this day, the beaches and cliffs around Lyme Regis in southwestern England, UK, are known for their rich fossil finds. They are part of the Jurassic Coast, a protected area that has perfectly preserved records of prehistoric times. This was the birthplace of Mary Anning, who would go on to become one of the world's most important paleontologists.

were hard. The Annings barely managed to get by until, in 1820, a professional fossil collector called Thomas Birch decided to help. He sold off his own fossil specimens and gave the proceeds of the sale to the family. Thomas felt the Annings deserved a better life because of their contributions to science.

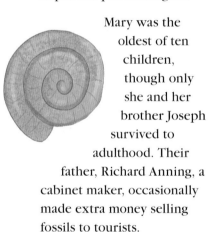

Mary was the oldest of ten children, though only she and her brother Joseph survived to adulthood. Their father, Richard Anning, a cabinet maker, occasionally made extra money selling fossils to tourists.

In 1810 Richard died, leaving his wife and children with debts to pay and no income. They began to collect fossils to support themselves. Mary had a particular knack for finding, extracting, and preparing them. Her mother, also called Mary, ran the business side of things. Times

Most of Mary's finds and sales were ammonites and belemnites—prehistoric molluscs that were common in the area. In 1811, however, the 12-year-old Mary presented London's scientific community with its first Ichthyosaurus. She went on to find more ichthyosaurs, the first complete plesiosaur (long-necked sea reptile), and Britain's first pterosaur (flying reptile). Mary was single-minded when she was fossil hunting and often put herself in danger. In 1833 she nearly died in a landslide that killed her dog, Tray.

"The world has used me so unkindly, I fear it has made me suspicious of everyone."

Even though many of Mary's specimens ended up in museums, it took a while for the mostly male scientists to give Mary any credit. They couldn't believe that a self-taught woman had any insights worth paying attention to.

Eventually, Mary's expertise could not be ignored. In 1838 the British Association for the Advancement of Science, along with the Geological Society of London, awarded Mary a yearly income. She was also made an unofficial member of the all-male Geological Society.

Mary changed the face of geology, established the field of paleontology, and raised important questions about Earth's history. At the time, the Bible's story of creation in seven days was widely accepted. Mary's work, along with research by Charles Darwin and others, contributed to a new scientific, evidence-based theory—evolution.

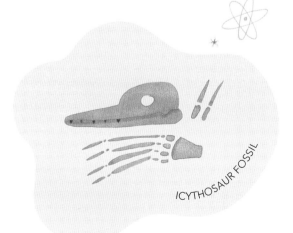

ICYTHOSAUR FOSSIL

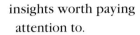

MARIE CURIE
CHEMIST AND PHYSICIST

(1867–1934)

Marie Curie (born Maria Skłodowska) grew up in Warsaw, Poland. Her parents were both teachers and she was their fifth and youngest child. The family did not have much money and were even poorer after Marie's mother died in 1878.

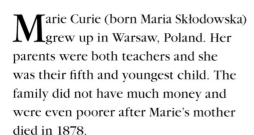

Polish universities did not accept women. Marie worked as a governess to support her sister, Bronisława, who was studying medicine in Paris, France, and to save up for her own fees for a French university.

Marie arrived in Paris in 1891. She took a degree in physics at the Sorbonne, then a second degree in mathematics. She met fellow scientist Pierre Curie and the two married in 1895. Marie began to study uranium rays for her PhD.

Marie and Pierre invented a device called the gold leaf electroscope which could measure the radioactivity of substances placed between the electrodes. By 1898 they had found two new radioactive elements—polonium (named after Marie's birth country) and radium. Marie came up with the term "radioactive." In the next few years she published many research papers, some with Pierre. She was the first woman in Europe to gain a doctorate in science.

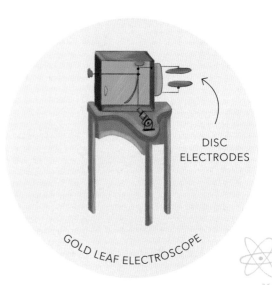

DISC ELECTRODES

GOLD LEAF ELECTROSCOPE

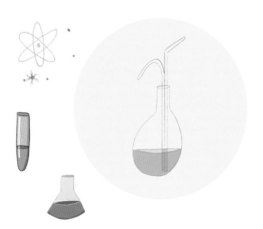

In 1903 Marie and Pierre won the Nobel Prize in Physics for their work on radioactivity. They shared it with physicist Henri Becquerel, who had first seen radioactivity. The following year the Curies presented their findings on curing cancer with radiation therapy.

In 1906 Pierre was tragically run over and killed by a horse-drawn cart. The Sorbonne offered his job to the heart-broken Marie. She accepted and became the university's first female professor.

Marie had been the first woman to win a Nobel Prize. In 1911 she became the first person to be awarded two, this time in chemistry. She had developed a method for measuring radioactivity. That same year, she was made director of the Sorbonne's new radioactivity laboratory, which had been named after her. She also ran the Institute for Radioactivity in Warsaw.

In World War I Marie put X-ray machines in ambulances and field hospitals. X-ray imaging at the front line sped up medical diagnosis and saved many soldiers' lives.

In 1934 Marie died of a rare disease caused by all the radiation she had been exposed to over the years. She had not realized the danger. Even today Marie's notebooks are so radioactive that people have to wear protective clothing to handle them.

"Nothing in life is to be feared; it is only to be understood."

HEDY LAMARR

INVENTOR AND ACTOR

(1914–2000)

Hedy Lamarr was born Hedy Kiesler in Vienna, Austria. When she was 19, she married an arms dealer who had ties to German Nazis and Italian Fascists. Hedy, however, was Jewish. When it became clear that World War II (1939–45) was unavoidable, she divorced her husband and left Europe.

In 1938 Hedy boarded a ship to the United States, bound for Hollywood and a career as an actor. She already had a signed contract with MGM Studios after meeting the film producer Louis B. Mayer in Paris the previous year. Hedy became famous, and starred in big-budget films. She went on to be one of Hollywood's first female producers, creating some groundbreaking work.

"All creative people want to do the unexpected."

Working with American composer George Antheil, Hedy devised a secure communications system for warships to control their torpedoes. It used radio signals that kept switching frequency so they could not be tracked or jammed. Hedy and George's wireless system was a forerunner of GPS, Wi-Fi, and Bluetooth.

Beyond the Hollywood success, Hedy had an unusual hobby— she loved inventing things. She developed her most important invention during the war, when she was just 27 years old.

In 1995, aged 80, Hedy's work was recognized with the BULBIE Gnass Spirit of Achievement Award, the "Oscars of invention."

GERTY CORI

Biochemist

(1896–1957)

Born in Prague, now part of the Czech Republic, Gerty Cori (born Gerty Radnitz) decided aged 16 that she wanted to become a doctor. She worked hard to get into the university and studied medicine from 1914 to 1920. She met her husband Carl Cori at university—they married in 1920.

same amount of experience. The couple started investigating what happens to sugar after it has been eaten. They discovered how the body stores energy and releases it. This process is called the Cori cycle.

In 1947 Carl and Gerty were awarded the Nobel Prize for Physiology or Medicine for their work on the body's sugar storage and release. One result of their research was the development of new treatments for diabetes (a condition that affects blood sugar levels).

"I believe that in art and science are the glories of the human mind. I see no conflict between them."

The Coris moved to Vienna, Austria, after Carl got a job at the university. As a woman, Gerty was not allowed an academic job. She had to take an assistant position at a hospital. After two years, the couple decided to emigrate to the United States.

Gerty and her husband started working as researchers in Buffalo, New York. Gerty was employed a few ranks below Carl, even though she had the

SYLVIA EARLE
Marine Biologist

(b.1935)

In 2016 President Barack Obama of the United States made an important announcement—he was expanding the protected area of ocean around the Hawaiian islands to make it the largest section of that type on Earth. This landmark decision was thanks to the work of Sylvia Earle (born Sylvia Reade), one of the world's most influential marine scientists.

Sylvia moved to the Gulf of Mexico with her family when she was 12. It was here, witnessing ocean wildlife close up, that she discovered her love for the marine environment. She started diving in 1953 and later completed two degrees in botany, carrying out extensive research into algae.

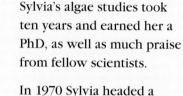

Sylvia's algae studies took ten years and earned her a PhD, as well as much praise from fellow scientists.

In 1970 Sylvia headed a mission as part of Project Tektite, where teams of four scientists and an engineer lived in an underwater laboratory for up to 20 days. Sylvia's all-female team carried out important research and also captured the American public's imagination—the women were praised for their dedication and bravery.

Sylvia used her newfound fame to speak out about pollution in the oceans. She had seen first-hand the damage caused by plastic waste, chemicals, and overfishing. She became a tireless campaigner for the protection of what she called "Earth's blue heart."

Sylvia also pushed the boundaries of deep-sea diving. In September 1979 she descended 381 m (1,250 ft) to the seabed—a world record for an untethered (unattached) dive. She walked for two hours in her heavy, high-tech suit, exploring depths that no diver had ever seen before.

In 1982 Sylvia co-founded a submersible company. It designed Deep Rover, a bubble-shaped, one-person research submarine that gave an all-round view and could descend to 1,000 m (3,300 ft).

Sylvia has served on national marine boards, led more than 50 expeditions, published over 100 scientific papers, and written books about protecting the world's oceans. In 1998 she became the National Geographic Society's first female Explorer-in-Residence, a position she still holds today.

"Even if you never have the chance to see or touch the ocean, the ocean touches you with every breath you take, every drop of water you drink, every bite you consume."

DEEP ROVER

In 2009, Sylvia founded Mission Blue, which has the aim of creating Hope Spots—areas of protected ocean that are a refuge for marine wildlife. In Hawaii, that mission has been accomplished.

VALENTINA TERESHKOVA
COSMONAUT (SOVIET ASTRONAUT)

(b.1937)

VOSTOK 6

Valentina Vladimirovna Tereshkova was born in a village 265 km (165 miles) northeast of Moscow, Russia (then part of the Soviet Union). Her father, who had been a tractor driver, was killed in. Times were tough for Valentina, her mother, and two siblings. Valentina left school at 16 to work in the same factory as her mother. However, she also continued to study by taking distance-learning courses.

Valentina's passion was skydiving. She joined her local flying club and made her first parachute jump at the age of 22. She trained every weekend. She performed jumps by day and by night, over grasslands, mountains, and rivers.

In 1961 Valentina applied to join the Soviet space program, which had plans to put the first woman in space. There were more than 400 applicants, but Valentina was one of the five who were chosen, thanks to her skydiving skills. The other four were all test pilots. The young women had months of training, followed by exams to see which of them would go into space.

In 1963 26-year-old Valentina was chosen for the mission. Her spacecraft *Vostok 6* launched in June.

Valentina stayed in space for three days and orbited Earth 48 times. During the flight, she took photographs of our planet which later helped scientists to understand features of its atmosphere. She also communicated via radio with fellow cosmonaut Valery Bykovsky. He was flying solo, too, on *Vostok 5*, which had been launched two days before Valentina's spacecraft.

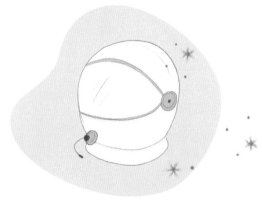

Valentina returned to Earth a national hero, an international icon for women's equality, and a campaigner for peace. She has often spoken about how humbling and overwhelming it was to see Earth from space—"a planet at once so beautiful and so fragile."

Valentina was asked to lead an all-female crew on *Voskhod 2* in 1965, but the mission was called off for technical reasons. Four years later, the female cosmonaut unit was broken up. To her disappointment, Valentina never went into space again. Instead, she has held many high-level jobs in government. She travels the world giving talks, opening exhibitions, and calling for

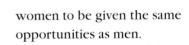

"Anyone who has spent any time in space will love it for the rest of their lives. I achieved my childhood dream of the sky."

women to be given the same opportunities as men.

Valentina has received the UN Peace Medal and many other awards, been made a

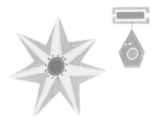

"Hero of the Soviet Union," and had a moon crater and minor planet named after her. If there is ever a Mars mission, Valentina wants to be part of it: "I am ready," she has promised.

RUCHI SANGHVI
ENGINEER

(b.1982)

Born in Pune, India, Ruchi Sanghvi was told by her father early in life that business was "a man's world." Determined to prove him wrong, Ruchi went to study in the United States. Even though she had never even touched a computer, she studied electrical computer engineering. She was one of five female students on the course out of a total of 150.

In 2005 Ruchi joined Facebook as its first female software engineer. She introduced some of its most successful and innovative features, such as the News Feed. Ruchi went on to found her own company, become an investor, and co-found the campaign group FWD.us. The group aims to improve immigration procedures, promote better education, and champion advances in technology.

WANG ZHENYI
Scientist, Astronomer, and Poet

(1768–97)

Unlike most girls in 18th-century China, Wang Zhenyi was lucky enough to receive an education. She grew up in eastern China with her father, grandfather, and grandmother, who were all scholars. They introduced Wang to mathematics, medicine, geography, and astronomy. Later she also learned archery, riding, and martial arts.

Wang wrote more than a dozen books in her short lifetime. She studied the moon, sun, and their eclipses, rewrote mathematics texts to make them easier to understand, and also wrote her own poetry. For centuries her work was not widely appreciated, but in 2004 a crater on Venus was named after her.

MÁRIA TELKES
SCIENTIST AND INVENTOR

(1900–95)

Born and educated in Budapest, Hungary, Mária Telkes moved to the United States in 1924 and took a job as a biochemist. She helped to invent a device that could record brain waves. From the late 1930s Mária focused on solar energy and how to harness it. She developed one of her most important inventions during World War II—a solar-powered contraption that could turn seawater into drinking water.

After the war, Mária worked with architect Eleanor Raymond to create the first house that was heated by solar energy. Throughout her career, Mária continued to develop pioneering solar technologies, including stoves and heaters. In 1952 she received the first Society of Women Engineers Achievement Award.

ADA YONATH
Biochemist and Crystallographer

(b.1939)

Ada Yonath was born in Jerusalem, Israel, the daughter of Polish immigrants. The family was poor and Ada's father died when she was 11, so she had to help out a lot at home. Even so, she graduated from school and attended university, becoming a biochemist.

In the 1970s Ada began to study ribosomes—small but important proteins inside animal cells. She was told that it was impossible to see them in any detail, so she came up with a new technique. She found that she could take X-ray images of the atoms inside ribosomes if she chilled them to incredibly low temperatures. In 2000 Ada and her team were able to announce their success. Ada's work has been incredibly important for the development of new antibiotics. In 2009 Ada and two of her fellow scientists were awarded the Nobel Prize in Chemistry.

GRACE HOPPER
Computer Scientist and Naval Officer

(1906–92)

She was known as "Amazing Grace," the "First Lady of Software," and the "Mother of Computing." Without Grace Hopper's decades of work, computers would still need highly trained professionals to program them, and groundbreaking scientific leaps such as spaceflight might never have happened.

Grace was born in New York City, USA. Her father, who owned an insurance

"It is often easier to ask for forgiveness than to ask for permission."

company, wanted his daughter to have the same opportunities as his two sons. Grace was privately educated and went on to complete two degrees in mathematics and physics and a PhD in mathematics.

When the United States joined World War II in 1941, Grace wanted to do her bit for the war effort. Her grandfather had been a rear admiral, but she couldn't join the Navy because of her age. She was accepted into the US Naval Reserve instead. In 1943 Grace was sent to Harvard University, Massachusetts, to take part in a top-secret naval project.

The team at Harvard was working on the Mark I, one of the earliest computers. It was designed to perform the long calculations that warships use to fire their weapons accurately. Grace was one of the Mark I's three programmers and wrote its 561-page instruction manual. She even coined the computing term "bug," after a moth got stuck in the machine and caused havoc.

MARK I

In 1949 Grace went to work on UNIVAC I, the first commercial electronic computer. She also developed the first compiler—the component that translated the numbers and symbols fed into a computer into the zeros and ones that told the machine what to do.

In 1955 Grace wrote FLOW-MATIC, the first computer language that used English words and phrases instead of complex mathematical symbols. It was the basis

MICROCHIP

for COBOL—a commonly accepted language that could program computers made by different manufacturers. Grace advised the committee that decided on COBOL and promoted it tirelessly. By 1970 it was the world's most widely used computer language.

Grace was still working in her sixties and seventies. She standardized the many computer languages being used in the Navy and was one of the first women to reach the rank of rear admiral. She finally retired in 1986, just a few months before her 80th birthday.

In 1991 US President George Bush Senior awarded Grace the National Medal of Technology and Innovation. It was just one of many awards and prizes given to this groundbreaking computer scientist.

CHIEN-SHIUNG WU
EXPERIMENTAL PHYSICIST

(1912–97)

Chien-Shiung Wu was fortunate enough to attend one of the first schools in China that allowed girls. Her parents had founded the school and were teachers there.

When Chien-Shiung was ten years old, she went to a boarding school 80 km (50 miles) away. She loved physics and mathematics and went on to study both subjects at university. She graduated from the National Central University in Nanjing in 1934 with the highest marks in her year.

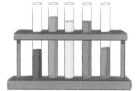

Chien-Shiung decided to complete her PhD in the United States. She arrived in San Francisco in 1936 and was offered a place at Berkeley, California, which had a world-famous physics department. Chien-Shiung's supervisor had invented a particle accelerator and she used it to split uranium and xenon atoms and produce radioactive isotopes. (An isotope is a version of an element that has the usual number of proton particles but a different number of neutrons.)

Chien-Shiung met fellow physicist Luke Yuan at Berkeley, and they married in 1942.

In 1944 Chien-Shiung went to work on the Manhattan Project, which was building the first atomic bomb. She was part of the team turning uranium metal into enriched uranium—radioactive isotopes that could fuel a nuclear reaction. She also helped to fix a problem with one of the project's nuclear reactors.

In 1945 Chien-Shiung became a professor at Columbia University, New York City. She became an expert on beta decay—a particular kind of radioactivity during which beta rays are released.

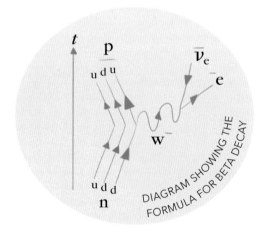

DIAGRAM SHOWING THE FORMULA FOR BETA DECAY

Chien-Shiung's biggest achievement was disproving the law of conservation of parity—a theory that scientists had believed to be true for decades.

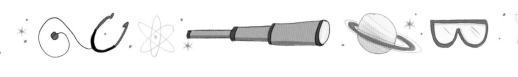

Two male colleagues, Tsung-Dao Lee and Chen-Ning Yang, predicted this law did not always apply. In late 1956 Chien-Shiung led a team of scientists to set up her complex and famous Wu Experiment that proved her colleagues were right. In 1957 Lee and Yang were awarded the Nobel Prize for their contribution to particle physics.

Although Chien-Shiung was not a Nobel Prize winner, she received an impressive number of scientific prizes and other distinctions during her lifetime. In 1978

she was the first winner of the Wolf Prize in Physics.

Chien-Shiung retired in 1981 but she continued to travel and give talks on the importance of women in science.

"There is only one thing worse than coming home from the lab to a sink full of dirty dishes, and that is not going to the lab at all!"

CHAPTER 3

ARTISTS
AND
WRITERS

Art is part of being human. It includes visual arts, such as painting, photography, and film; literary arts, including novels, poems, and plays; and performing arts, such as music, drama, and dance. In all its forms, art helps us to explore our identity and express feelings and big ideas.

Great artists can be men or women, but in many cultures success has been easier for men. Women authors have even chosen to write under male names to increase their chance of being published and read.

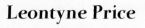

George Eliot's real name, for example, was Mary Ann Evans.

Being poor can make it harder to be an artist. Having music lessons, going to the ballet, or being able to access lots of books all cost money. As a result, the arts can lack voices from their most disadvantaged members—but thankfully there are exceptions.

Leontyne Price

(b.1927)

Soprano singer Leontyne Price was the first African American to be a leading artist at the Metropolitan Opera in New York City, USA. She had to overcome many obstacles. Leontyne's 1961 debut at the Met was greeted with more than 40 minutes of non-stop applause.

Jane Austen

(1775–1817)

Since the 19th century, Jane Austen has been one of Britain's most popular novelists. Her works, which include *Pride and Prejudice* and *Emma*, have been turned into films and television series many times. Jane's witty words described life for women in the middle and upper classes and drew out truths that are still relevant to this day.

The women in this chapter are writers, poets, singers, musicians, designers, painters, and actors. Many of them came to their art because they needed to express themselves and their position in society. Being an artist and an activist often go hand in hand. Women have harnessed the power of art to comment on society, challenge wrong or harmful ideas, and nudge or catapult us toward change.

NINA SIMONE
Musician, Singer, and Activist

(1933–2003)

Nina Simone (born Eunice Kathleen Waymon) was from North Carolina, USA. Her mother was a Baptist minister and her father was a maintenance person and preacher. Nina was only three years old when she started playing songs on the organ in her mother's church.

Recognizing her incredible talent, Nina's parents sent her to piano lessons. She was a natural and decided to become the first black classical pianist. Her home town raised money to fund her time at high school and then Juilliard, New York City's leading school for music and dance.

Nina grew up at a time of terrible racial discrimination. Slavery had been abolished in 1865, but many states, especially southern ones, had

"You can't help it. An artist's duty, as far as I'm concerned, is to reflect the times."

segregation. Black citizens weren't allowed to share public spaces with white people. The civil rights movement in the 1960s worked to change this through peaceful protests and campaigning.

Being exposed to unfairness and racism throughout her life shaped Nina as an artist. When she was 12 years old, she gave her first-ever piano recital. Her parents, who were seated in the front row, were asked to move to make space for white audience members. Nina refused to play until her parents were given back their seats.

Nina gave up her hopes of becoming a classical pianist in 1951, when she was rejected by the prestigious Curtis Institute of Music in Philadelphia. It was a disappointment, but it led to Nina's amazing career as one her century's most celebrated musicians and singers.

In 1954 Nina started working as a musician in a bar. She adopted the stage name "Nina Simone" to keep her mother from finding out—she wouldn't have approved! Nina's rich voice and her soulful versions of much-loved songs made her a popular fixture.

Nina released her first album in 1958. It was a big success but she had sold the creative rights to the record company. None of the profits went to her. In the 1960s Nina joined the fight for civil rights and sang songs at rallies.

Frustrated by the racism in the United States, Nina spent most of the 1970s in Barbados, Africa, and Europe. In 1987 she reached a new generation when her recording of "My Baby Just Cares for Me" accompanied a high-profile perfume advertisement. In 1991 Nina published her autobiography, *I Put a Spell on You*. She spent the last 10 years of her life in southern France. Thanks to her extraordinary voice and accomplished piano playing, Nina has inspired many young musicians.

SONITA ALIZADEH
Rap Artist and Activist

(b.1997)

In 2014 the film-maker Rokhsareh Ghaemmaghami started documenting the lives of refugees in her native Iran. She met a teenager called Sonita Alizadeh, who had fled her home country of Afghanistan when war broke out there. Rokhsareh began filming Sonita. As a result, she caught on camera the moment when Sonita's mother said she had found a husband to buy her.

"To the women of my beloved country: believe in yourselves. You are strong. Speak up about your dreams and your goals every day so that everyone knows that you exist"

Although the sale of brides is common in Afghanistan, Sonita was shocked that it was going to happen to her. She was just 16 years old. She expressed her fear and despair in a rap song called "Brides for Sale." Rokhsareh filmed the video for the song. When it was uploaded to YouTube, "Brides for Sale" went viral.

Rokhsareh paid Sonita's family to delay the marriage and helped her travel to Utah, USA, where a high school was offering her a scholarship. The Strongheart Group, which is dedicated to social change, also gave Sonita financial support. She continues to raise awareness of child marriage.

Rokhsareh's film *Sonita* was released in 2016 and won an award at the Sundance Film Festival in Park City, Utah.

JOAN ARMATRADING
MUSICIAN, SINGER, AND SONGWRITER

(b.1950)

When Joan Armatrading was 14, she saw a second-hand guitar in a shop window and begged her mother to buy it. Her mother swapped two baby strollers for it, and Joan became the proud owner of her first guitar. She taught herself to play and started writing songs. Within two years she was playing her first gig.

Born on the Caribbean island of Saint Kitts, Joan moved to Birmingham, UK, with her family when she was seven years old. Her musical talent was evident early on, when she started playing her mother's piano as a young child. Once she discovered the guitar, she embarked on a lifelong career as a singer, songwriter, and musician.

In 1972 Joan released her debut album and became the first black British female artist to find success with her own material. Since then she has released more than 20 solo albums. Her records have gone gold (sold 500,000 copies) and platinum (sold a million). She has been nominated for three Grammy Awards and two Brits.

In 2001 Joan was made a Member of the Order of the British Empire (MBE). She gained a history degree the same year. Joan supports many charities, especially ones that help young people.

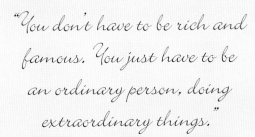
PLATINUM RECORD

"You don't have to be rich and famous. You just have to be an ordinary person, doing extraordinary things."

ANNE FRANK

WRITER

(1929–45)

Born into a Jewish family, Anne Frank spent the first years of her childhood with her parents and older sister Margot in the German city of Frankfurt. When dictator Adolf Hitler came to power in 1933, Jewish people were suddenly discriminated against. The Frank family moved to Amsterdam in the Netherlands to avoid persecution.

The family soon settled. Anne's father Otto started his own business, the girls

went to a local school, and Anne's mother Edith took care of the house. As war loomed, the Franks tried to emigrate but they were too late. Germany invaded Poland and World War II began.

In 1940 German troops marched into the Netherlands. Once more the Frank family faced anti-Semitic (anti-Jewish) laws. Margot and Anne had to attend schools for Jewish children and their father had to give up his business. Otto tried again to move his family to the United States, but it was just not possible.

In 1942 Otto built a hideout behind a bookcase at the back of his shop. The family planned to go into hiding in mid July, but they brought the date forward after receiving a letter for Margot from the German government. It told her she must return at once to Germany and report to a work camp. Later that year four more Jewish people joined them in their secret hiding place.

Only six trusted friends knew where the family was. They had all worked for Anne's father. They kept the Franks safe, brought them food, clothing, and books, and were their only contact with the outside world.

Anne kept a diary that documented her experiences. She wrote about everyday life in hiding, composed short stories, and collected quotes that she liked.

Life continued in this way until 1944 when someone informed the authorities. The Gestapo (Nazi secret police) raided the

building, found the hideout, and arrested everyone. Anne and Margot were transported to Bergen-Belsen concentration camp; their parents were separated and sent to Auschwitz.

Otto was the only member of the family who survived the war. When he returned to Amsterdam his friend Miep Giess gave him Anne's diary, which she had found after the raid and kept safe. Otto was deeply moved by his daughter's writing and decided to publish it.

Since that time Anne Frank's diary has been translated into more than 70 languages and sold more than 30 million copies. It is one of the most powerful and moving pieces of wartime literature ever written.

"I still believe, in spite of everything, that people are really good at heart."

KIRI TE KANAWA
Opera Singer

(b.1944)

New Zealander Kiri Te Kanawa, who is part-Maori, was taught to sing at high school. She shot to fame in 1971 with a part in *The Marriage of Figaro* at the Royal Opera House in London, UK. One of Kiri's proudest moments during a long and successful career was being heard by more than 600 million people worldwide when she sang at the wedding of Prince Charles and Lady Diana Spencer in 1981. She was made a Dame Commander of the Order of the British Empire (OBE) in 1982.

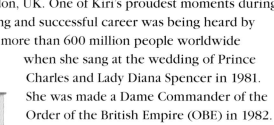

ROYAL OPERA HOUSE

Kiri retired from singing in 2017 to focus on the Kiri Te Kanawa Foundation. She set up this organization in 2004 to support and teach talented young singers from New Zealand.

ANGELINA JOLIE
ACTOR AND ACTIVIST

(b.1975)

Angelina Jolie Voight was born in Los Angeles, USA. She made her screen debut at age seven in a movie starring her father, actor Jon Voight, but her breakthrough role was in *Hackers* (1995). Angelina won her first Golden Globe in 1998 and picked up an Oscar in 2000.

Angelina is a humanitarian activist as well as a successful actor. When she was a UN Goodwill Ambassador she trained as a pilot so she could deliver aid to refugee camps. In 2012 Angelina was given diplomatic powers when she became a UN Special Envoy. She is also involved in community development, promoting human rights, and conserving habitats.

NADEŽDA PETROVIĆ
Painter

(1873–1915)

Born in Čačak, Serbia, Nadežda Petrović showed promise as a painter when she was still a teenager. She trained as an art teacher and then studied in Munich, Germany, where she met up-and-coming artists including Paul Klee and Wassily Kandinsky. Her first solo exhibition took place in Belgrade in 1900. Over the next decade or so, Nadežda made a name for herself for her impressionist and wild style.

When the Balkan Wars (1912–13) broke out, Nadežda volunteered as a nurse with the Red Cross and earned a Medal for Bravery. She had to stop in 1913 after catching typhus and cholera. Nadežda also served as a nurse with the Serbian army in World War I until she died of typhus in 1915.

MELBA LISTON
MUSICIAN

(1926–99)

Born in Kansas City, Missouri, USA, Melba Liston came from a musical family. She started to teach herself the trombone when she was seven years old and joined her school band. Within a year she was performing a solo on the local radio. When Melba was ten the family moved to Los Angeles, and she began to have private trombone lessons.

Melba began her career as a professional trombonist when she was 16. She toured with successful big band masters such as Dizzy Gillespie and earned respect in the male-dominated world of jazz. In later life Melba was a composer, arranger, and producer for soul-music artists including Marvin Gaye and The Supremes.

MIRIAM MAKEBA
SINGER AND ACTIVIST

(1932–2008)

When Zenzile Miriam Makeba was born, no one could have believed that she would grow up to be one of the first African singers to find international fame. Her home was a poor black township on the outskirts of Johannesburg, South Africa, and her parents were from different ethnic backgrounds—her father was Xhosa and her mother was Swazi.

When Miriam was only six years old, her father died suddenly. She had to take on cleaning and babysitting jobs to help to make money for the family. Miriam had already discovered her musical gift and was singing in the choir at school and church. She grew up believing that music would lift her out of poverty one day.

In 1948 the South African government introduced apartheid, a system to keep white and black people separate. Good homes and jobs were not on offer for black people like Miriam. They could not even share public spaces with white people.

Miriam became a professional singer in the 1950s. She toured southern Africa with a group called the Manhattan Brothers and also formed her own all-female group called the Skylarks.

In 1958 Miriam had a role in an anti-apartheid film called *Come Back, Africa*. It wasn't a big part, but she sang in it—and audiences loved her voice.

Miriam flew to New York City, USA, and found jobs singing in jazz bars. A

calypso singer called Harry Belafonte became her mentor and encouraged her to make her first recordings.

"Girls are the future mothers of our society, and it is important that we focus on their well-being."

In 1960 the South African police shot at black protestors in a township called Sharpeville. They killed 69 people and injured 220. Miriam's mother died in the massacre. Miriam tried to return to home for her mother's funeral, but she discovered that she had been banned. It was the start of 31 years in exile.

It was an extraordinary time to be black and living in New York City. The African-American civil rights

movement was at its peak. Miriam became involved, but above all she spoke out against apartheid in her home country. At the same time, her musical career was taking off.

In 1990 Miriam returned to South Africa. Apartheid was now outlawed and the anti-apartheid activist Nelson Mandela had been released after 27 years in prison.

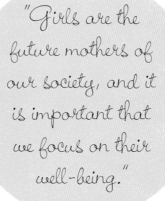

Known as "Mama Africa," Miriam became a Goodwill Ambassador for the UN in 1999 and was awarded the Otto Hahn Peace Medal in Gold in 2001. She died in Italy during her farewell musical tour.

BJÖRK

Musician, Singer, and Actor

(b.1965)

Known only by her first name, Björk Guðmundsdóttir was born in Reykjavik, Iceland. Her musical career started early—she recorded her first solo album at 11 years old and spent her teens in various bands. From 1986 to 1992 Björk was in a group called the Sugarcubes, which found fame in the UK and the United States.

Björk launched her solo career in 1993. With a singing style unlike anyone else's, Björk is not afraid to experiment and the results can be soaringly beautiful. Björk also has a strong interest in the visual arts and her stage shows are extraordinary spectacles. She won the Best Actress Award at the 2000 Cannes Film Festival.

MIXING DECK

In 2010 Björk released an album called *Biophilia*. It featured a new instrument called the Sharpsicord (an automatic accoustic harp), but there was something even more groundbreaking about it. Björk had collaborated with scientists, teachers, app developers, and even an Icelandic choir to create an interactive version. The *Biophilia* app gives users hands-on understanding of music theory and science, is simple to use, and creative.

SHARPSICORD

It is now used in schools in Iceland, Finland, Norway, and Sweden.

Björk cares about the environment and protecting Iceland's landscape. She also supports people around the world who are fighting for their independence.

"If you want to make something happen that hasn't happened before, you've got to allow yourself to make a lot of mistakes."

VIRGINIA WOOLF
Writer

(1882–1941)

Adeline Virginia Stephen grew up in a large, unconventional family. Although she didn't have much formal schooling, she read everything and anything in her father's huge library. Virginia's family spent winters in London, UK, and summers in their house on the Cornish coast, southwestern England. Both locations appear in her writing.

women face in a society where men hold all the power.

Sadly Virginia suffered with mental illness her whole life. In 1941 she felt she could no longer go on, and she committed suicide.

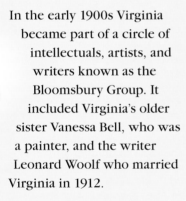

In the early 1900s Virginia became part of a circle of intellectuals, artists, and writers known as the Bloomsbury Group. It included Virginia's older sister Vanessa Bell, who was a painter, and the writer Leonard Woolf who married Virginia in 1912.

The Woolfs founded Hogarth Press in 1917 and it went on to publish Virginia's novels *Mrs Dalloway* (1925) and *To the Lighthouse* (1927). Both were groundbreaking, as they experimented with language, and the order in which the story was told. Her work made a huge contribution to literature, and influenced many future writers.

She went on to write *A Room of One's Own* (1929). Here she described the difficulties

"If you do not tell the truth about yourself you cannot tell it about other people."

FRIDA KAHLO

PAINTER

(1907–54)

Magdalena Carmen Frida Kahlo y Calderón was born in Coyoacán, Mexico. Her father was German and her mother had mixed Spanish and indigenous ancestry. While growing up, Frida spent a lot of time with her father, who was a photographer. She developed a keen eye for detail and took painting classes, but her real ambition was to be a doctor.

Frida's life changed in 1925 when she was involved in an accident—the bus she was on crashed into a streetcar and Frida nearly died. It took her months to recover. While she was stuck in bed, she started to paint in earnest, mostly portraits of family, friends, or herself.

In 1927 Frida joined the Mexican Communist Party (PCM). She met the artist Diego Rivera, also in the PCM, the following year. He was 21 years older than Frida and famous for his huge murals, which were inspired by Mayan art. Frida showed him her paintings and he encouraged her to be an artist.

Influenced by Diego, Frida began to celebrate her Mexican heritage. She wore traditional dress and introduced

XOLO (SHORT FOR XOLOITZCUINTLI), A SACRED HAIRLESS DOG

elements of folk art to her paintings, such as bright textures, bold patterns, and flattened shapes.

In 1929 Frida and Diego married. They spent their first few years of marriage in the United States where Diego was painting. In 1933 they moved back to Mexico City. Their home was perfectly

STREETCAR, MEXICO CITY

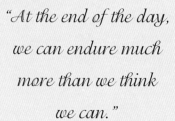

"At the end of the day, we can endure much more than we think we can."

Frida spent her last years in extreme pain because of damage from the 1925 accident. She wore steel corsets and had lots of operations. In the end, she could not stand or walk, but she still painted.

Frida left behind many great artworks. She expressed her Mexican culture and above all she explored difficult feelings, such as pain, from a female viewpoint.

suited to their stormy relationship. It was actually two houses—one for each of them—joined by a bridge. The couple had no children but kept a menagerie of pets including monkeys, parrots, and xolos—hairless dogs that had been kept by the ancient Maya and Aztecs.

In 1938 Frida had her first solo exhibition in New York City, USA. She was finding international success as an artist, but her marriage to Diego was crumbling. They divorced in 1939 and Frida moved back to her childhood home, where she created some of her most vulnerable paintings.

In 1940 Frida and Diego remarried and they stayed married until her death.

SIMONE DE BEAUVOIR
Writer and Philosopher

(1908–86)

In the early 1900s many French girls grew up hoping to marry well, rather than earn money for themselves. It was traditional for brides to enter marriage with a sum of money called a dowry. Those from prosperous families had larger dowries, so they could be choosier about who they married.

Simone de Beauvoir was born into a middle-class family in Paris. Her father lost most of the family fortune just after World War I. Rather than making Simone hunt for a husband with a pitiful dowry, he decided to spend the little money they had on her education.

The family lived very frugally and their sacrifices paid off. Simone enjoyed studying and had a sharp mind. In 1929 she left the Sorbonne university in Paris with a degree in philosophy.

For the next 14 years Simone supported herself by teaching. She worked in high schools in Marseille, Rouen, and Paris. In 1943 her first novel, *She Came to Stay*, was published

and Simone was finally able to become a full-time writer.

Simone is best known not for her novels but for her philosophical work *The Second Sex* (1949), which became a global bestseller. She argued that through history societies had treated women as a "second sex," expecting

THE SORBONNE

them to live and behave in a way that suited the interests of men. As wives and mothers, women put the needs of their husbands and children before their own. Simone called for a future where men and women were treated as equals.

Simone lived by the ideas in *The Second Sex*. She met the philosopher Jean-Paul Sartre while she was at university and they had a lifelong relationship. They never married, shared a home, or had children. They read each other's work and went on trips together. They also agreed that each of them was free to have relationships with other people. They gave each other plenty of space and time so they could write and focus on their careers. Jean-Paul died in 1980 and Simone in 1986. They are buried side by side.

Over the years, Simone produced an impressive number of works, including short stories, essays, travel diaries, and an autobiography. Her 1954 novel *The Mandarins* won the Prix Goncourt for its imaginative writing. In 1975 Simone won the Jerusalem Prize, which is awarded to people who write about freedom.

In the 1970s she became involved in the feminist movement. She took part in demonstrations, wrote articles, and signed open letters that demanded more rights for women. Simone's greatest gift to women was showing that they can live however they choose and need to be responsible only for themselves.

"I am too intelligent, too demanding, and too resourceful for anyone to be able to take charge of me entirely."

JOANNE (J. K.) ROWLING
Writer, Film Producer, and Philanthropist

(b.1965)

Joanne Rowling was born near Bristol, in southwest England, UK. She loved reading from a young age and made up stories for her younger sister, including one about a clever giant rabbit.

Not long after Joanne left university her mother died of multiple sclerosis (MS). She went to teach in Portugal, married, and had a baby. In 1993 she left her husband and moved to Edinburgh.

With no job and a daughter to look after, Joanne decided to write. She did this in local cafés because the baby used to fall asleep on the way. Joanne finished writing *Harry Potter and the Philosopher's Stone* in 1995. Twelve publishers rejected it before Bloomsbury published it in 1997.

Today Joanne is the world's most successful author. Her *Harry Potter* series has been translated into 65 languages, turned into movies and a musical, and won numerous awards. Joanne was inspired to write a spin-off series, *Fantastic Beasts*. She has also written novels for adults. In 2000 Queen Elizabeth II made her an Official of the Order of the British Empire (OBE) for her services to children's literature.

"It is impossible to live without failing at something, unless you live so cautiously that you might as well not have lived at all—in which case, you fail by default"

OBE

Joanne is also a philanthropist. She uses her vast wealth to help disadvantaged children, support single parents, fund MS research, and much more.

XIAN ZHANG
CONDUCTOR

(b.1973)

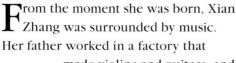

From the moment she was born, Xian Zhang was surrounded by music. Her father worked in a factory that made violins and guitars, and he later owned a music shop. Her mother had trained as a pianist.

Xian's mother started to teach her piano when she was three years old. By the time she was six, Xian was playing up to eight hours a day. At 13 years old she left her home city of Dandong, China, to study music in Beijing. She wanted to be a concert pianist, but her teacher at the conservatory (music school) said her hands were too small. She decided to be a conductor instead.

Xian was just 19 the first time she led an orchestra. Her teacher encouraged her to conduct a rehearsal at the Central Opera House in Beijing. Xian did such an outstanding job that she was asked to come back.

In 1998 Xian went to the United States to study for her PhD in Cincinnati, Ohio. In 2002 she won the first Maazel–Vilr

"I was lucky in that what my parents wanted me to do and trained me for was what I wanted to do."

Conductor's Competition, which was founded to support up-and-coming conductors. She joined the New York Philarmonic Orchestra as sick cover and went on to be associate conductor.

Since then, Xian has been in demand all over the world. She has conducted in Milan, Amsterdam, Dresden, London, Cardiff, and New Jersey. In the very male world of conducting, she is an inspiration.

ARUNDHATI ROY
WRITER AND ACTIVIST

(b.1961)

Suzanna Arundhati Roy was born in Assam, northeastern India. Her Hindu father ran a tea plantation. Her mother Mary was from a Syrian Christian community in Kerala, southern India.

When Arundhati was two years old, her parents separated and her mother moved back to Kerala with the children. Arundhati's grandparents had disapproved of their daughter's mixed

marriage to a Hindu and they turned her away. Mary took the children to a cottage her father owned 150 km (90 miles) away. It was a time of hardship. Their mother was ill, so Arundhati and her older brother had to beg for food. They returned to Kerala three years later and Mary became a teacher.

Arundhati went to boarding school at ten, then moved to Delhi when she was 16. She had no money and lived in

slums. Arundhati studied architecture because she wanted to know how to design cheap, sustainable housing, but she became downhearted and eventually chose to be a writer instead.

Arundhati had an acting part in *Massey Sahib* (1985), a film about mixed marriage and discrimination directed and written by Pradip Krishen. Arundhati went on to collaborate with Pradip on scripts for a television series and a couple of films.

In 1997 Arundhati's first novel, *The God of Small Things*, was published. Written as a series of flashbacks, it told the story of a twin brother and sister growing up in Kerala. They witness violence and injustice because of the caste system (the Indian way of grouping the people in society by race). Its character Velutha is an "Untouchable" from the lowest caste.

In 1997 *The God of Small Things* won the Man Booker, a prize that had never been awarded to an Indian woman before. Arundhati donated her prize money and royalties to human rights charities.

To her readers' surprise, Arundhati did not publish another novel for 20 years. After experiencing hopeless poverty as a

girl, Arundhati was sensitive to society's treatment of its most vulnerable citizens. In the booming Indian economy, new money was often made by exploiting the poor or damaging the environment— and it almost all ended up in rich people's pockets.

"If you ask me what is at the core of what I write, it isn't about "rights," it's about justice. Justice is a grand, revolutionary, beautiful idea."

Arundhati's political writings exposed the dangers of greed and globalization and supported issues such as Kashmiri independence. In 2004 she was awarded the Sydney Peace Prize and in 2014 she was on the *Time* list of the 100 Most Influential People in the World. Arundhati's long-awaited second novel, *The Ministry of Utmost Happiness*, appeared in 2017.

MAYA ANGELOU
Writer, Singer, Actor, and Activist

(1928–2014)

To this day, *I Know Why the Caged Bird Sings* can be found on many school and college reading lists. An account of Maya Angelou's childhood, it illustrates the painful reality of African-American life in the early 1900s.

Born Marguerite Annie Johnson in St. Louis, Missouri, Maya was sent to rural Arkansas with her brother when she was three years old. Her parents had divorced, and her father wanted the children to live with his mother.

Arkansas was segregated at that time, which meant that black citizens could not share the same public spaces

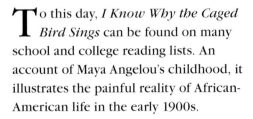

"It's one of the greatest gifts you can give yourself, to forgive. Forgive everybody."

as white people and were regularly discriminated against. Schools put black children at a disadvantage.

Maya's autobiography described a distressing incident that happened when she was eight years old. She was abused by a family friend. Maya was brave enough to tell someone and her attacker was caught, tried, and imprisoned.

Unfortunately he was released a day later and murdered. Maya felt so guilty about his death that she didn't speak for five years. She finally found her voice again thanks to help from a kind woman called Mrs. Flowers.

Maya moved to San Francisco with her mother and brother when she was 14. While she was still finishing school she worked on the streetcars. She was the city's first black female conductor. Maya had a baby son when she was 17, just after leaving school.

When she was 20 years old, Maya started training as a dancer and decided to use her nickname "Maya" as her professional name. She toured Europe in musicals and found roles in plays in New York City.

From 1961 to 1965 Maya spent time in Egypt and Ghana. When she returned

to the United States she became involved in the civil rights movement.

Maya worked closely with the civil rights leaders Martin Luther King, Jr. and Malcom X. When Martin Luther King, Jr. was assassinated in 1968, Maya was devastated. She put her energy into writing.

I Know Why the Caged Bird Sings, published in 1969, was one of seven autobiographies that Maya wrote during her lifetime. Some of Maya's fans believe that these are her most important works because they look at black identity.

Maya's first collection of poems appeared in 1971 and was nominated for a Pulitzer Prize. The following year Maya became the first African-American woman to have written the screenplay for a feature film. In 2011 President Barack Obama presented Maya with the Presidential Medal of Freedom.

PRESIDENTIAL MEDAL OF FREEDOM

LAVERNE COX
ACTOR AND ACTIVIST

(b.1972)

Laverne Cox is a successful actor, producer, writer, and activist. She is transgender, meaning that her identity and gender is not the same as her birth sex. She was *Time* magazine's first openly transgender cover star and one of the first in the transgender community to find worldwide fame.

Laverne was born in Alabama, USA, and raised by her mother and grandmother. She was bullied at school for appearing feminine. Laverne found acting fame in 2013 when Netflix broadcast the first season of *Orange is the New Black*. She played the transgender inmate and prison hairdresser Sophia. Laverne travels widely to raise awareness and talk about how racism and poverty make life even more difficult for people in LGTBQ+ communities.

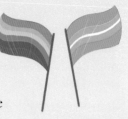

MARIA CALLAS
Opera Singer

(1923–77)

Maria Callas was born in New York City, USA, to Greek parents. When she was 13, she moved to Athens, Greece, with her mother and older sister. The great Spanish soprano Elvira de Hidalgo taught her to sing and after World War II suggested that she move to Italy. Maria built up her career there. By the 1950s she was performing in the world's leading opera houses, including La Scala in Milan, the Royal Opera House in London, and the Metropolitan Opera in New York City. Maria stopped singing live in 1965.

Maria's voice divided opinion. Some said that she sang like an angel, while others criticized her technique and "wobbly" high notes. She could also be difficult to work with. But everyone agreed that she brought opera to life like no other.

MILLO CASTRO ZALDARRIAGA
DRUMMER

(b.1922)

Growing up in Cuba in the 1920s and 1930s, Millo Castro Zaldarriaga, a young girl of Cuban, Chinese, and African heritage, dreamed of being a bongo player. The drums were an important part of Cuban culture, just as they are today. But at that time only boys and men were allowed to play them. Millo's father refused to pay for her to have lessons but she was so persistent that he eventually gave in.

Millo formed an all-girl band when she was ten, played at American President Franklin D. Roosevelt's birthday party at 15, and later toured the world as a jazz musician. Millo had rhythm, talent, and determination—but above all, she had the courage to follow her dreams.

GRACE COSSINGTON SMITH
Painter

(1892–1984)

Born Grace Smith in Sydney, Australia, Grace studied art in England and Germany as well as her home city. She became an artist when most painters were men. Grace's style of painting was post-impressionist—it emphasized the basic shapes of figures and scenery and used striking shades and thick brushstrokes to capture the effects of the light. Her 1915 work *The Sock Knitter* is Australia's first post-impressionist painting.

Grace painted many pictures of Sydney, including the building of its iconic bridge. Her work was admired by other painters, but ignored by the critics. In 1973 Grace was given an Order of the British Empire (OBE). She admitted that she was glad she hadn't received much attention during her career because it had allowed her to focus on how she wanted to paint.

COCO CHANEL
FASHION DESIGNER AND BUSINESSWOMAN

(1883–1971)

The "little black dress," the neat tweed suit, the quilted purse, and the costume pearl necklace … all of these timeless "classics" have one thing in common. They were designed by the groundbreaking fashion designer Coco Chanel.

Born Gabrielle Bonheur Chanel in Saumur, western France, Coco's spent her childhood in poverty. When she was 12, her mother died of tuberculosis. Coco and her two sisters were sent to a convent, while their brothers became farmhands.

Coco learned to sew at the convent. When she left aged 18, she went to work as a seamstress and bar singer in the city of Moulins. It was around this time that she took the name "Coco."

Coco made some rich friends in Moulins, including the French socialite Étienne Balsan and English polo player Boy Capel. These men helped her to fund her first businesses: a hat shop that she opened in Paris in 1910 and a clothing boutique in the fashionable seaside resort of Deauville in 1913.

> *"The most courageous act is still to think for yourself. Aloud."*

At the time women were expected to wear long frilled dresses in heavy fabrics, over tight, restrictive corsets. Coco wanted to make simple, elegant clothing in comfortable fabrics and she drew her inspiration from menswear. Her sailor's clothes and shorter skirts gave women more freedom and captured the spirit of the time.

Coco's boutique was a runaway success and she soon opened stores in Biarritz and Paris. By 1919 she was a registered couturier (fashion designer).

One of Coco's biggest successes was Chanel No. 5, the perfume that she launched in 1922. No fashion house had released its own branded scent before. Chanel No 5 was also the first mass-produced perfume with multiple "notes" rather than a single scent. It is still a bestseller today.

In 1926 Coco created the little black dress—a simple dress suitable for any occasion. Coco was responsible for making black—associated with mourning—chic and fashionable. It was perfect for showing off strings of large, fake pearls and other accessories.

By the late 1930s the House of Chanel had 4,000 employees. Coco closed her business at the start of World War II and did not reopen until 1954. She updated her tweed suit, launched the "hands-free" Chanel bag with its long strap of gold chain, and rescued women from high heels with her flat, two-tone ballet pumps.

Coco died in 1971, but her bold ideas lived on. She revolutionized fashion and the Western woman's wardrobe, giving them clothes that suited their new, active lifestyles.

ZAHA HADID
Architect

(1950–2016)

When Zaha Hadid died suddenly in March 2016, it wasn't just fellow architects who mourned. Zaha's inspirational, monumental, and unique buildings had shaped cities and landscapes all over the world. Her creations were part of people's lives. Unusually for an architect, Zaha had made the leap from unconventional outsider to famous and "mainstream" in a very short space of time.

HEYDAR ALIYEV CENTER, AZERBAIJAN

Zaha was born in Baghdad, Iraq. Her family were Sunni Muslims and she was one of three children. Her father was a prominent politician who believed in democracy and social reform; her mother was an artist. Zaha went to schools in Baghdad, England, and Switzerland. She gained a degree in mathematics from the American University of Beirut, Lebanon.

As Zaha was growing up, she became interested in architecture. It was a time of great optimism, when forward-thinking architects were rebuilding cities after the devastation of World War II.

In 1972 Zaha moved to London, UK, to study at the Architectural Association (AA). Her tutors included the architects Rem Koolhaas and Elia Zenghelis, who were known for their daring and intelligent work. The AA had a reputation for radical architecture that looked amazing on paper but was not actually buildable. Zaha excelled there but, unlike many fellow students, she wanted to construct her creations.

Zaha opened her own architectural firm in London in 1980. One of her first projects was a small fire station on the German–Swiss border. Its dramatic, sloping concrete walls at irregular angles and large, frameless windows catapulted her to fame. Today the building is used for art exhibitions.

Over Zaha's career, technology improved and materials could be used in new ways. Zaha refined her trademark style, creating curvy buildings such as the London Aquatics Centre for the 2012 Olympic Games and the Heydar Aliyev Center, an arts complex in Azerbaijan.

LONDON AQUATIC CENTRE

In 2004 Zaha became the first woman to win the prestigious Pritzker Architecture Prize, which recognizes architects who show great vision and talent. In 2010 she was awarded the Royal Institute of British Architects (RIBA) Stirling Prize for the MAXXI, a museum of modern art and architecture in Rome, Italy. She was made Dame Commander of the Order of the British Empire (OBE) in 2012.

Zaha proudly collected the RIBA Royal Gold Medal just eight weeks before her sudden heart attack. She was the first woman to receive the prize, which acknowledges a lifetime of great architecture.

"Yes, I am a feminist, because I see all women as smart, gifted, and tough."

CHAPTER 4

ATHLETES
AND
ADVENTURERS

History books are packed with real-life male action heroes—explorers, generals, spies, and sports stars—but where are the female ones? Many women have excelled in these areas, often against all odds.

The energetic high-achievers in this chapter went above and beyond to prove their power. Whether they were floating in space, scaling a mountain, steering a faulty plane over the ocean, or redefining a whole sport, they faced challenges with courage. They believed in themselves, and that made anything possible.

Sometimes these women risked their lives for their ideals. Some crossed enemy lines with fake identities to help their countries win a war—and they all refused to shrink their ambitions to fit silly notions of feminine frailty. Some overcame disabilities to win medal after medal in Paralympian sports—showing us, in the process, that physical prowess has a lot to do with attitude. By boldly ignoring all those restrictive rules about what women can and cannot do, these extraordinary role models have opened up the world to us all.

Ida Pfeiffer

(1797–1858)

Born in Vienna, Austria, Ida dreamed of far-off places after a childhood trip to Palestine and Egypt. Her globetrotting began late in life when she was a 45-year-old widow. Ida journeyed around the world twice. Her trips could last months or even years and she paid for them by publishing her travel journals. She also sold specimens of animals, plants, and minerals.

Vera Atkins

(1908–2000)

Born in Romania, Vera emigrated to Britain in 1937 and became a key secret agent of World War II. Her job was recruiting spies to gather intelligence in France. Vera was dedicated to her work and had a strong sense of duty. After the war she visited France in person to find out what had happened to British agents who went missing there.

MARTA

SOCCER PLAYER

(b.1986)

Far in the northeast of the country, Alagoas is one of Brazil's most disadvantaged states. More than one-fifth of its people cannot read or write; the hospitals are understaffed and overcrowded; its industries are declining; and water supplies and sanitation are limited.

Marta Vieira da Silva was born and grew up in Alagoas. Her father left when she was a year old, and her mother went out to work full-time as a cleaner.

Home alone with her two brothers and sister, Marta discovered soccer. She played out on the street without shoes and kicked a ball made of scrunched-up plastic bags. When Marta was five, her mother refused to buy her a ball, saying "You're a girl, Marta." But Marta did not accept that soccer was just for boys. By the age of seven, she was training with the boys every day.

Marta couldn't attend school regularly because of her family's money problems. From the age of 11, she worked as a street vendor selling fruit and clothes and also played for her local soccer club.

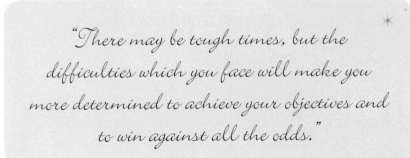

"There may be tough times, but the difficulties which you face will make you more determined to achieve your objectives and to win against all the odds."

When Marta was 14 years old, she was talent-spotted by soccer scout and coach Helena Pacheco. Marta made a three-day bus trip to Rio de Janeiro to join the Vasco da Gama club.

Marta represented Brazil in the 2002 under-20 Women's World Cup and she moved up to the national squad the following year. She was voted Fifa Women's World Player of the Year five years running from 2006 to 2010.

In the 2007 Women's World Cup Marta won the Golden Ball for best player and Golden Boot as top scorer. She has won silver medals in two Olympics and was disappointed to be knocked out in the semi-finals at the 2016 Rio Games.

Marta has played for clubs in Europe and the United States, as well as Brazil. She reached the final of the UEFA Women's Cup (now the Women's Champions League) twice with Swedish club Umeå IK.

Marta is considered the best female soccer player in history, celebrated for her skill, speed, and finesse. She had to be tough to make it in Brazil, a country where the women's game was banned from 1941 to 1979 for being unfeminine.

FIFA WOMEN'S PLAYER OF THE YEAR

Women's soccer still faces huge inequality. A 2017 survey found that top male player Neymar, who is from Brazil like Marta, earned the same as all 1,693 players in the top seven women's football leagues combined. His salary from Paris Saint-Germain FC was 1,150 times more than Marta's from Orlando Pride. There is still a long, long way to go.

VENUS WILLIAMS
TENNIS PLAYER

(b.1980)

Long before Venus Ebone Starr Williams was born, her father Richard dreamed of having a child who was a tennis star. He saw the sport as a path out of poverty—a way to break free from the ghetto. He and his wife Oracene learned all about the game from books and videos. When their four-year-old daughter Venus showed promise, they began to coach her on local public

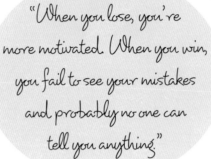

"When you lose, you're more motivated. When you win, you fail to see your mistakes and probably no one can tell you anything"

courts. Soon Venus's younger sister Serena joined in the training. The girls gave each other support and healthy competition.

By the age of ten, Venus could serve a ball at 160 km/h (100 mph), and at 14 she took up tennis professionally. Venus's debut at the US Open was in 1997. She ranked only 66th in the world but reached the final—the first unseeded player to do so.

In 2000 Venus won two Grand Slams (Wimbledon and the US Open) and two Olympic gold medals (for the women's singles and doubles) in Sydney, Australia.

Venus stayed at the top of her game for years in spite of injuries and having to cope with an autoimmune disease. She wasn't the first African American to win a Grand Slam—Althea Gibson achieved that in 1956—but she ushered in a new, powerful way of playing. Venus succeeded by trusting her own individuality—and that makes her an example for people in all walks of life, not just tennis.

WIMBLEDON TROPHY

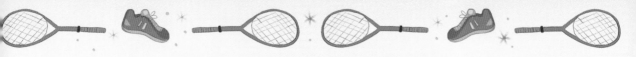

SERENA WILLIAMS
Tennis Player

(b.1981)

Born 15 months after her sister Venus, Serena Jameka Williams has profited from her parents' determination to make their daughters tennis stars. She was included in her sister's training sessions, and the girls started entering tennis tournaments when Serena was age five.

One year after Venus became a professional player, Serena followed in her footsteps. She went on to win the US Open in 1999—a year before her big sister. However, her real breakthrough year was 2002, when she won a Grand Slam hat-trick—the French Open, US Open, and Australian Open.

Winning the Olympic gold and all four Grand Slam tournaments is known as a Career Golden Slam. In 2002 Serena became the second woman to achieve one in the singles (Steffi Graf was the first). Playing in the doubles, the Williams sisters have completed *two* Career Golden Slams!

Serena's win at the 2017 Australian Open took her total Grand Slam singles titles to a record-breaking 23. The victory was all the more extraordinary because she was eight weeks pregnant at the time.

Like Venus, Serena plays with a forceful, athletic style. Her career has been inspirational, especially to young black players. Serena and her sister have been trailblazers for much-needed diversity in the sport.

"The success of every woman should be the inspiration to another. We should raise each other up."

AUSTRALIAN OPEN TROPHY

BESSIE COLEMAN
Aviator

(1892–1926)

Texas, USA, still had segregation laws when Bessie Coleman was born there in 1892. It was nearly 30 years since slavery had been abolished, but many white people still held racist views and often treated black people as inferior.

Bessie was the tenth of 13 children. Her father was mixed-race (Cherokee and African-American) and her mother was African-American. They were farmhands. Bessie helped out in the fields, but she also had an education. She went to a segregated school and had one term at the African-American university in Langston, Oklahoma.

When she was 23, Bessie went to live in Chicago and worked as a nail technician. She became fascinated by flying.

Newspapers were full of stories about the brave pilots returning from World War I. Aviation was still very new. The first powered flight had only happened in 1903.

No American flying school would take Bessie because she was mixed-race and a woman. She got the idea of going to France, where there was less discrimination, from Robert Abbott, who ran Chicago's biggest black newspaper. He and Jesse Binga, owner of Chicago's first African-American bank, helped to fund Bessie's trip.

Bessie went to the best flight school in France at Le Crotoy. Aircraft were dangerously flimsy in those early days and some of Bessie's fellow students died during training.

In June 1921 Bessie earned her international pilot's license. She was the first black woman pilot. Bessie decided to make a living as a "barnstormer" or stunt pilot. Barnstorming was a popular entertainment in the 1920s.

On 3 September 1922 Bessie took part in an air show on Long Island, New York. It was the first of many. A skilled and dedicated pilot, Bessie wowed audiences

QUEEN
BESSIE

"The air is the only place free from prejudices."

by flying upside down, rolling, diving, and looping-the-loop. She became known as "Queen Bessie."

Bessie wanted to break down racial barriers. She refused to perform to segregated audiences and she also gave talks about aviation to African Americans in churches, halls, and schools. She was saving up to start the first black flying school when she tragically died on in April 1926. She fell to her death during a rehearsal for a stunt show and her mechanic also died in the accident. Thousands came to Bessie's funeral to pay their respects. To this day, African-American pilots mark the anniversary of her death by flying over her grave and dropping flowers.

Bessie's dream of a black flight school did become reality. In 1929 African-American army pilot William Powell opened the Bessie Coleman Aero Club in Los Angeles.

YUSRA MARDINI
SWIMMER

(b.1998)

A gifted swimmer from Damascus, Syria, Yusra Mardini became an Olympic athlete against all odds. After the Syrian Civil War broke out in 2011, Yusra's home city was repeatedly bombed. Still, she continued to train and in 2012 she represented her country at the World Swimming Championships.

Three years later, Yusra and her sister fled Syria. When the engine of the boat carrying them broke down, they jumped into the sea and pushed it, together with another refugee. Their heroic swim to safety took more than three hours. The Mardini sisters eventually found a new home in Berlin, Germany. In 2016 Yusra competed at the Olympic Games in Rio, Brazil. Although she didn't win a medal, her story was an inspiration to people everywhere.

TEREZINHA GUILHERMINA
Sprinter

(b.1978)

Often described as the fastest blind woman in the world, the Brazilian Paralympian Terezinha Guilhermina was born with a disease that slowly destroyed her eyesight. Five of her 12 brothers have the same condition.

When Terezinha was 22, she joined a training scheme for disabled athletes in her home city of Betim. At first she swam, because she couldn't afford running shoes. After her sister gave her a pair, Terezinha took up sprinting. Since then she has competed in four Paralympic Games and achieved world records for different races in her category T11, which is for totally blind athletes. She sprints blindfolded, alongside a sighted guide runner.

KRYSTYNA SKARBEK
WARTIME SPY

(1908–52)

Known as Winston Churchill's "number one spy," Krystyna Skarbek (who later changed her name to Christine Granville) was a Polish countess. She moved to Britain after Germany invaded her country in September 1939, causing the outbreak of World War II. Determined to join the fight against Germany, Krystyna entered the British Secret Service or SOE. She was its first female special agent and its longest serving one.

Krystyna was brave, daring, and dedicated to protecting her new home country. On one mission she skied out of German-occupied Poland with evidence that the Nazis were planning to invade Soviet Russia hidden in her glove. She also helped in the fight to free France. Krystyna was awarded the George Cross, an OBE, and the Croix de Guerre for her courage and service.

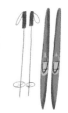

ANNE BONNY
Pirate

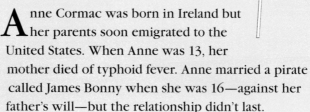

(c.1698–c.1782)

Anne Cormac was born in Ireland but her parents soon emigrated to the United States. When Anne was 13, her mother died of typhoid fever. Anne married a pirate called James Bonny when she was 16—against her father's will—but the relationship didn't last.

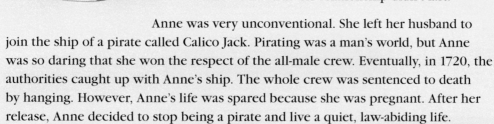

Anne was very unconventional. She left her husband to join the ship of a pirate called Calico Jack. Pirating was a man's world, but Anne was so daring that she won the respect of the all-male crew. Eventually, in 1720, the authorities caught up with Anne's ship. The whole crew was sentenced to death by hanging. However, Anne's life was spared because she was pregnant. After her release, Anne decided to stop being a pirate and live a quiet, law-abiding life.

AMNA AL HADDAD
WEIGHTLIFTER

(b.1989)

A simple walk in the park changed Amna Al Haddad's life. She was 19 at the time, suffering from depression, and taking antidepressants. She ate junk food, never exercised, slept 12 hours a day, and didn't have any friends. Amna is open about how she felt: "I was at one of the lowest points in my life, with no hope that the future could be better."

She couldn't go on as she was, so Amna decided to change. She went for a walk around nearby Safa Park on the outskirts of her home city, Dubai, United Arab Emirates (UAE). Amna's next step was to join a gym. As soon as she tried weightlifting, she loved it. It was perfect for making her more resilient (able to bounce back). As Amna's physical health improved, so did her mental wellbeing.

Building up her strength wasn't Amna's biggest challenge. Dubai has a strict code of conduct based on Islamic laws. For a long time it was taboo for women to take part in sports. They were only allowed to be weightlifters from 2000. Amna had such passion for her chosen sport that she was ready to challenge convention and show that Muslim women can be powerful athletes.

By 2012—just five years after taking up weightlifting—Amna was ranked 77th out of 170 women in Asia after she competed in the Reebok Crossfit Games Open. She set herself an ambitious goal—to represent the UAE in the 2016 Rio Olympics.

Amna gave up her job as a journalist to be a full-time weightlifter. Whenever she competed, she made headlines. She was often the only Emirati to compete or the first woman in a hijab.

In 2015 Amna won six gold and three silver medals in the International Weightlifting Federation (IWF) Asian Interclub Championships. Nike offered her a sponsorship deal and she worked

with the brand to develop its first sport hijab. Amna applauded Nike for making sports more accessible to Muslim girls and women who chose to wear the hijab as a sign of modesty. At the same time, she also made it clear that she supported all Muslim sportswomen—whether they wore the hijab or not.

Amna qualified for the Rio Games, but had to pull out because of an injury to her lower back. However, her example has inspired more Muslim women and girls to follow their dreams. Through her honesty, Amna has removed some of the stigma around depression. She is also living proof that exercise is a fantastic way to improve mental health.

"Women have the right to choose what to wear as athletes, and religious beliefs should never be a barrier to pursuing sports."

JESSICA WATSON
Sailor and Writer

(b.1993)

In May 2010 thousands of people gathered at Sydney Harbour, Australia, to welcome home an extraordinary teenager. Sailor Jessica Watson, then 16 years old, was returning from a 210-day solo journey around the world. She was the youngest person to sail non-stop around the world.

"You don't have to be someone special to achieve something big. You just have to have a dream, believe in it, and work hard."

Some people criticized Jessica's parents for letting her go, especially since she had crashed into a freighter (large ship) during a test run. There were also concerns about how Jessica would cope with being alone for so long.

In 2011 Jessica was named Young Australian of the Year. She is a Youth Ambassador for the United Nations' World Food Programme (WFP), which works to end hunger.

Jessica faced challenging moments. During one especially vicious storm, the wind picked up her yacht *Ella's Pink Lady* and threw it into the base of a towering wave. The boat was knocked onto its side at least seven times during the journey.

Jessica wrote a blog, which was read by people around the globe. She documented her difficulties, but also described the amazing wildlife she encountered. The supportive messages that she received from her followers really helped to boost her morale. After she returned home, Jessica wrote a book about her experiences called *True Spirit*.

MARINA RASKOVA
War Pilot and Navigator

(1912–43)

When Marina Malinina was growing up in Moscow, Russia, she dreamed of following in her father's footsteps and becoming an opera singer. But her ambitions changed while she was at school and she focused on chemistry instead. Marina left high school in 1929, seven years after her country had become part of the Soviet Union. Marina worked as a chemist in a dye factory, met an engineer called Sergei Raskov, and married.

In 1931 Marina went to work for the Soviet Air Force. She became its first female navigator. In 1934 Marina became the first woman to teach at the Zhukovsky Air Academy in Moscow. She also set many long-distance flying records. In 1938 Marina was one of the first women to receive a Hero of the Soviet Union award.

After World War II had started, Marina called for women to be allowed to fly as military pilots. As a result, the women's flying corps was formed. It was made up of three regiments, each containing about 400 women—mechanics, engineers, and navigators, as well as pilots.

MARINA RASKOVA URGES THE SOVIET LEADER JOSEPH STALIN TO ALLOW WOMEN PILOTS, SEPTEMBER 1941:

"You know, they are running away to the front all the same—they are taking things into their own hands—and it will be worse, you understand, if they steal planes to go."

Marina commanded the dive-bombing regiment until she died in battle in 1943. She was given a state funeral in recognition of her bravery, and was later awarded the Order of Patriotic War 1st Class.

GERTRUDE BELL

Diplomat, Spy, Archaeologist, Mountaineer, and Writer

(1868–1926)

Gertrude Margaret Lowthian Bell was born into a wealthy family in County Durham, England. Her mother died when she was three years old, and her father remarried when she was seven. Gertrude's parents encouraged her to go to university, which was unusual at the time. She studied modern history at Lady Margaret Hall, one of Oxford University's first women's colleges, and was awarded a first-class degree.

In 1892 Gertrude visited her uncle, who was a British diplomat in Tehran, Persia (now Iran). She learned to speak Persian before her visit. While she was there she translated a book of Persian poetry into English and wrote her first travel book, *Persian Pictures*.

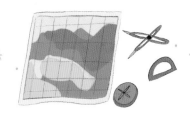

Gertrude became a keen and fearless climber. In 1902 she became stuck in a blizzard while scaling the highest peak in the Swiss Alps, the Finsteraarhorn. She earned the respect of mountaineers after she survived dangling off a rope for two days. The 2,632-m (8,635 ft) Gertrudespitze is named after her.

Gertrude learned the language wherever she went, got to know the local politics, and wrote letters home about what she did and saw. Over her lifetime, Gertrude became fluent in eight languages. She also taught herself archeology and was involved in digs in the Ottoman Empire (in the middle of which is now Turkey), Syria, and Mesopotamia (now Iraq). She was becoming an expert on the Middle East.

During World War I, Gertrude worked for the British Intelligence office in Cairo, Egypt, along with TE Lawrence ("Lawrence of Arabia"). Her familiarity with Arabic language, culture, and politics meant she could influence the events in the region to suit the British government.

> "It's so nice to be a spoke in the wheel, one that helps to turn, not one that hinders."

The British had encouraged Arabs in the region to revolt against Ottoman rule. After the war Gertrude was one of the experts who sat on the panel to decide the new borders within the territory. She was a driving force behind the creation of Iraq and its first king in 1921.

NATIONAL MUSEUM OF IRAQ

In 1923 Gertrude stepped down from politics and diplomacy to focus on another passion—archeology. Between 1923 and 1926 she established what is now the National Museum of Iraq and was its first director. Gertrude wanted the Iraqis to be able to keep archeological finds from the Sumerian, Babylonian, and Assyrian civilizations in their own country.

Gertrude is relatively unknown in her home country now, but she is held in high esteem in Iraq. After her death in 1926 she was buried in Baghdad and her grave there has been visited ever since. Many families in the Iraqi capital refer to Gertrude fondly as the "first lady of Iraq."

MiSTY COPELAND
PRiNCiPAL BALLERiNA

(b.1982)

Combining athleticism, technique, and emotion, ballet is incredibly demanding. Countless dancers strive to become professional, but only the tiniest number are successful. Among those is Misty Danielle Copeland, the first African American to be made principal dancer at the American Ballet Theatre (ABT) in New York City, USA.

Misty was born in Kansas City, but moved to San Francisco with her mother and five brothers and sisters when she was still very young. She never knew her father, and often struggled with her mother's partners. She lived in poverty.

When Misty was 13, she auditioned for the school dance team. After performing her own choreography, she was named the captain of the 60-strong squad. Her coach, who had a background in classical dance, recommended that Misty try some ballet classes.

Misty wasn't convinced that she would enjoy ballet, but she enrolled. For the first few weeks she had no clue what she was meant to be doing, but her instructor, Cindy Bradley, saw her huge potential at once.

Most professional dancers start training at the age of three. From her uncertain, late start, Misty progressed to attending

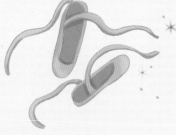

BALLET
BARRE

five classes a week. Within three months she could dance en pointe—a technique that takes most dancers years to master.

Cindy knew Misty's background was very poor, so she didn't charge to teach her ballet. When Misty's mother moved and it became impossible for her to travel back and forth between home, school, and ballet classes, Cindy invited Misty into her home during the week, and then Misty saw her mother on the weekends.

When Misty was 15, she won first place at the Los Angeles Music Center Spotlight Awards. Later that year she was awarded a full scholarship to the San Francisco Ballet's six-week summer course. In 1999 and 2000 Misty won scholarships to attend the ABT's summer school. She was one of six dancers (out of 150) who were asked to join the ABT's junior troupe. Misty soon rose to fame. In 2007 she became the ABT's first African-American soloist and in 2015 she became a

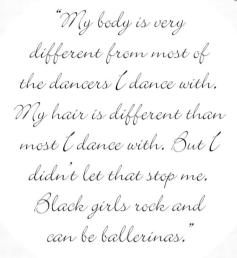

"My body is very different from most of the dancers I dance with. My hair is different than most I dance with. But I didn't let that stop me. Black girls rock and can be ballerinas."

THE NUTCRACKER

principal (the highest rank of dancer).

Misty has become an icon of popular culture. In 2016 she was the model for one of the Barbie "Sheroes" range. The doll wore a copy of the red unitard Misty wore in the ballet *Firebird*. Misty also starred in Disney's *The Nutcracker and the Four Realms* (2018) as the Ballerina.

Misty supports many charitable organizations and regularly mentors young dancers.

SACAGAWEA
EXPLORER AND INTERPRETER

(*c*.1788–1812)

Sacagawea was a Native American from the Shoshone tribe. When she was 11 or 12, she was captured by a party of the Hidatsa tribe and taken to their settlement. A few years later, the French-Canadian explorer and fur trader Toussaint Charbonneau bought Sacagawea and made her one of his many wives.

In 1804 the explorers Meriwether Lewis and William Clark hired Toussaint as a guide. They were going on an expedition to map the West for President Thomas Jefferson.

Meriwether and William asked Toussaint to bring along Sacagawea as an interpreter. They set off in March 1805, just a few weeks after Sacagawea had given birth to a son, Jean Baptiste. She carried her baby with her in a cradleboard.

> "Everything I do is for my people."

Sacagawea was a huge help on the expedition. As well as making it possible for the group to communicate and trade with the Shoshone, she could tell them which roots and plants were edible. She even made them moccasins to wear. On one occasion she rescued Meriwether and William's journals from a river.

Sacagawea is celebrated to this day. Numerous statues of her stand along the expedition trail. Her image also features on a collectable golden dollar coin produced from 2000.

MARY KOM
Boxer

(b.1983)

Nicknamed "MC Mary Kom" and "Magnificent Mary," Mangte Chungneijang Mary Kom was born in rural Manipur, a state in northeastern India. The oldest of three children, she helped her parents out in the rice fields. The family was very poor and sometimes they had nothing to eat.

When Mary saw footage of the legendary American boxer Muhammad Ali on television, she was inspired to take up the sport. She trained in secret, because her father had strict ideas about what girls should and shouldn't do.

"Don't let anyone tell you you're weak because you're a woman."

In 2000 Mary won the state boxing championship. Her father read about her victory in the papers, but he didn't start to accept and support her choice of career for another three years. Mary won her first World Amateur Boxing Championship in 2002 and her first Asian Women's Boxing Championship the following year.

In 2012 Mary became the first female Indian boxer to qualify for the Olympic Games. She returned home with a bronze medal, and went on to win gold in the 2018 Commonwealth Games.

Mary has set up an academy to teach boxing to children from poor backgrounds in Manipur and other parts of northeastern India. She also cares passionately about animal welfare.

OLYMPIC BRONZE

NOOR INAYAT KHAN
Writer and Spy

(1914–44)

In wartime, countries rely on spies—secret agents who adopt false identities, cross enemy lines, and find out inside information that might help win the war. Noor Inayat Khan was a fearless, intelligent, and conscientious spy who worked for Britain during World War II.

Born in Moscow, Russia, Noor was exposed to many cultures as she was growing up. Her father was an Indian Muslim and her mother was an American. During Noor's childhood, her family moved to London and then Paris, where her father died and Noor was educated. She studied music and medicine and was bilingual in French and English.

BIG BEN, LONDON

In 1939 Noor worked on a collection of Indian children's stories, which were published in the newspaper *Le Figaro*. When war broke out, she decided to train as a nurse with the French Red Cross. Shortly before France surrendered to Germany in November 1940, Noor fled to England with her mother and sister.

Noor's father, a Sufi mystic, had raised her to believe in peace and religious harmony. Noor was determined to work against fascist Germany and support

efforts to end the war. She joined the Women's Auxiliary Air Force (WAAF) in 1940 as a radio operator. She was soon noticed by Special Operation Executive (SOE) agents and recruited in 1942.

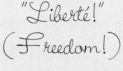

In 1943 Noor was sent to work for a resistance network in Paris. Her job was to radio any intelligence (information) back to London. Soon after she arrived many of the women in the network were arrested. Noor's bosses urged her to return home. However, she insisted on staying. She wanted to gather as much information as she could before she was found out.

EIFFEL TOWER, PARIS

"Liberté!"
(Freedom!)

NOOR'S LAST WORD
AS SHE WAS SHOT

Over the next three months, Noor ran the entire spy network. She had to keep moving and change her identity frequently. Eventually a double agent betrayed Noor and she was arrested by the Gestapo (German Secret Police.) She escaped, but was recaptured within hours. A month later, she was moved to a prison in Germany, where she was chained and kept in solitary confinement.

Despite repeated torture and starvation, Noor never volunteered any information to her captors. After ten months, she was moved to the concentration camp at Dachau, where she was killed by firing squad. After her death, Noor was awarded the Croix de Guerre and the George Cross for her bravery.

WAAF RADIO

CHANTAL PETITCLERC
Wheelchair Racer and Senator

(b.1969)

Until Chantal Petitclerc was 13 years old, her life was similar to that of many children in her home town of Saint-Marc-des-Carrières, Canada. Then one day Chantal was playing on a friend's farm when an old barn door fell onto her, breaking her spine.

When Chantal was released from hospital, she was in a wheelchair. She had lost the use of her legs because she was paralyzed from the hips down. Her physical education teacher offered her lunchtime swimming lessons to increase her upper body strength.

Chantal enjoyed the challenge and continued her swimming lessons until she graduated from school. Chantal went on to Université Laval in Quebec City,

where she was introduced to wheelchair athletics. She took part in her first competition and even though she came last, she was hooked. She continued to train while she completed her university studies and in 1992 she qualified for the Barcelona Paralympic Games. She brought home two bronze medals.

Over the next 16 years Chantal won more medals than any other Canadian track athlete or sportsperson. She was the only athlete to win gold medals in the Olympic Games, Paralympic Games, and Commonwealth Games. This was possible because wheelchair racing was included in the 2004 Olympics as well as the Paralympics.

Chantal has won a total of 21 Paralympic medals (14 golds) and broken 26 world records. In the 2004 Paralympics she won five gold medals—matching the record for a single Games (set by the Canadian swimmer Stephanie Dixon at the 2000 Paralympics). Chantal was chosen to carry the flag at the

> *"I believe in the power of sport to change lives, to make people better, and to empower."*

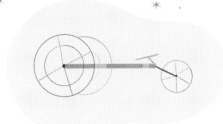

start of the 2006 Commonwealth Games, which took place in Melbourne, Australia.

Chantal retired from wheelchair racing after the 2008 Beijing Olympics. Since then she has been a coach and mentor for the British Paralympic teams and *Chef de Mission* (person in charge) for the Canadian teams at the Commonwealth and Paralympic Games.

Chantal is an ambassador for Right to Play, an international organization that educates children through play to help them overcome trauma and poverty. She also supports the Champions Fund, which gives grants to support promising Canadian female athletes, teams, and tournaments.

Chantal has been awarded honorary doctorates from universities across Canada and the Lou Marsh Trophy for Canadian Athlete of the Year. She was admitted into the Paralympic Hall of Fame in 2016. That same year, she started to serve as a senator for the Canadian government.

CANADIAN SENATE

ALEXANDRA DAVID-NÉEL
EXPLORER AND WRITER

(1868–1969)

Alexandra David-Néel was an adventurous child, often wandering off through the busy streets of her home city of Paris, France. She converted to Buddhism at 21 years old and this inspired her later travels across India, Japan, and China. In the winter of 1924 Alexandra crossed the Himalayas to Llasa, Tibet. The city was forbidden to foreigners, but she was able to enter it disguised as a beggar. Alexandra returned to Tibet in 1938 and studied Buddhism there for five years.

Alexandra lived to be almost 101. She spent the last 20 years of her life in France and Monaco writing about her travels. According to her wishes, her ashes were scattered in the River Ganges in Varanasi, India.

NATALIE DU TOIT
Swimmer

(b.1984)

STARTING BLOCK

Natalie du Toit was already a successful competitive swimmer when she lost the lower half of her left leg in a car accident at the age of 17. Determined to continue her sporting career, she returned to the pool after four months. She decided to compete as a Paralympian for her home country, South Africa.

Natalie was soon winning medals and breaking world records. In 2008 she was one of two Paralympians who qualified for both the Olympic and Paralympic Games. Over the course of her career, Natalie has won more than 18 gold medals. She retired from the sport in 2012.

JUNKO TABEI
MOUNTAINEER AND ENVIRONMENTALIST

(1939–2016)

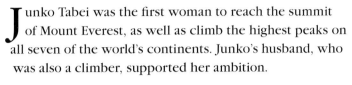

Junko Tabei was the first woman to reach the summit of Mount Everest, as well as climb the highest peaks on all seven of the world's continents. Junko's husband, who was also a climber, supported her ambition.

Junko founded Japan's first women's climbing club in 1969. Her ascent of Everest took place in May 1975. She continued to climb mountains till the end of her life. Junko worried about damage to Everest, so she returned to university in her sixties to complete a postgraduate degree in environmental science. She worked to protect and preserve delicate mountain environments.

MAJLINDA KELMENDI
Judoka (Judo Master)

(b.1991)

Majlinda Kelmendi is from Kosovo, a European state that was formed in 2008 from territory that had been part of Serbia. She started judo training at age eight. In 2009 she won the gold medal at the World Junior Championships in Paris.

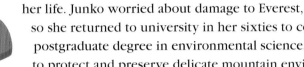

Majlinda took part in the 2012 London Olympics but she had to represent Albania—Kosovo was not yet recognized by the Olympic Committee. She achieved her first gold medal for Kosovo at the 2013 World Judo Championships. In the 2016 Rio Olympics Majlinda made history by winning Kosovo's first Olympic gold. She returned home a national hero. She has also won three gold medals in the European Championships. She competes in the 52-kg (115-lb) weight category.

AMELIA EARHART

AVIATOR

(1897–*c.*1937)

There are many competing stories about the end of American aviator Amelia Earhart's life. She and navigator Fred Noonan sparked a huge search when they went missing above the Pacific Ocean in July 1937. Not a trace of them was found—and no trace of the Lockheed Model 10-E Electra aircraft they were flying either. What happened to Amelia and Fred remains a mystery to this day.

Amelia was born in Kansas, USA. In 1917, just after starting university in Pennsylvania, she visited her sister in Toronto, Canada. Wounded soldiers were returning from World War I and Amelia was moved to help. Instead of returning to university, she volunteered at the military hospital.

In 1918 Amelia caught the Spanish flu that was sweeping across the world and would end up killing up to 100 million people. Amelia was hospitalized for two months and had to rest for almost a year. Amelia suffered from sinus problems for the rest of her life.

In 1920 Amelia went to live with her parents in California. It was here that she first flew in a plane. Amelia was so thrilled by the experience that she decided to take flying lessons. In 1921 her mother and sister helped her to buy her first plane, and by 1923 Amelia was a fully qualified pilot.

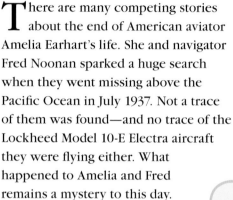

"The woman who can create her own job is the woman who will win fame and fortune."

In 1928 some promoters asked Amelia if she would be the first woman on a flight across the Atlantic Ocean. The plane was being piloted by two men so she would just be a passenger. Amelia agreed and returned a hero. She released a bestselling book, *20 Hrs 40 Min* (the time the flight took), went on a lecture tour across the United States, and was able to make money by being the "face" of various products and brands.

Wanting to justify her fame, Amelia made a transatlantic solo flight in 1932. She completed the crossing in record time, despite various difficulties along the way. This was the beginning of a series of record-breaking flights and historical firsts. In 1932 she became the first woman to receive the Distinguished

Flying Cross, and in 1935 she was the first person to fly solo from Hawaii to the US mainland.

Amelia was one of the pilots who founded the Ninety-Nines in 1929, an organization where women pilots offered each other mutual support. She also designed a clothing line for women who "lived actively."

DISTINGUISHED FLYING CROSS

When Amelia went missing, she had almost completed a pioneering round-the-world flight. She had packed a lot of living into her 40 years of life.

SIMONE BILES
GYMNAST

(b.1997)

Simone Arianne Biles is one of the most gifted gymnasts in sporting history. She is celebrated globally, but her road to success wasn't easy.

Born in Ohio, USA, Simone was two years old when she and three siblings were taken into foster care because their mother was struggling with alcohol and drug addiction. When she was six, Simone was adopted by her biological grandparents in Texas. Today she sees them as her parents.

Around this time Simone joined a gymnastics class after a teacher noticed her talent on a school trip. She was a natural and progressed very quickly.

Simone was spotted at the age of eight by the gymnastics coach Aimee Boorman, who has been her trainer ever since. Aimee has given Simone much-needed support, especially during the tougher phases of her training when she

SPRINGBOARD

"I'd rather regret the risks that didn't work out than the chances I didn't take at all."

struggled with flexibility and wasn't performing as well.

In 2011, when Simone was 14 years old, she had to make one of the biggest decisions of her life—did she want to become a full-time professional gymnast, training 32 hours over six days every week, or did she want to lead a regular teenage life and miss out on being an elite athlete?

VAULT

Determined to become a world-class gymnast, Simone opted for intensive training and home schooling. At first her results were outstanding, and she started to make a name for herself. But in 2013, she injured herself repeatedly during a championship, tripping, falling, and making mistakes. Aimee pulled her from the competition.

Simone's parents decided to enlist the help of a sports psychologist, who

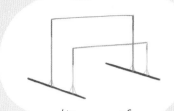

UNEVEN BARS

helped Simone work through what may have been anxiety about performing. An incredible three weeks later, she won the US Championships —two months after that she was awarded a world title.

Simone made history by becoming the first woman to win ten gold medals in the World Championships (across 2013, 2014, and 2015). She also holds the most World Championship medals of any American gymnast.

In 2016 Simone made her Olympic debut in Rio. She returned home with four gold medals (for the individual all-around, vault, floor, and team categories). She also won a bronze for the balance beam. Simone took a well-earned rest from training in 2017 before returning to the world of gymnastics in 2018.

As well as setting new, extremely high standards in gymnastics, Simone dedicates time to charities that are close to her heart. She wants children in foster care to have the support and opportunities to realize their potential. She also works with Kids Wish, which makes dreams come true for children with terminal illnesses.

GLOSSARY

ABOLITIONIST Someone who supported the banning of slavery.

ANNOTATION A note that explains a word or passage in a text.

ANTHROPOLOGIST Someone who studies the human race.

APARTHEID A system of racial segregation in South Africa (1948–93).

ARCHAEOLOGIST Someone who studies history through looking at objects from the past.

BIOCHEMIST A scientist who studies chemical reactions in organisms.

CELL One of the tiny units from which all living things are made.

CHROMOSOME A long molecule made of DNA.

CIVIL RIGHTS MOVEMENT The group of people who came together in the 1950s and 1960s to end racial inequality. It began in the United States.

CONCENTRATION CAMP A prison where civilians, especially Jews, were kept in very inhumane conditions and were often killed.

COSMOLOGIST Someone who studies the whole Universe.

CRYSTALLOGRAPHER Someone who studies the structure of crystals.

DEMOCRACY A system of government whereby the people have a say, usually by electing representatives.

DEPRESSION A mental condition that makes people feel hopeless and isolated, which affects energy, sleep, and appetite.

DISCRIMINATION An unfair system that treats people differently, for example because of their sex, race, sexuality, or age.

DNA A complicated chain of chemicals inside a cell with instructions for life.

EMPATHY The ability to share someone else's feelings.

ENTOMOLOGY The scientific study of insects.

ENVIRONMENTALIST Someone who wants to protect the natural world.

ETHOLOGIST Someone who studies animals in their natural habitat.

EXTREMISM Holding extreme religious or political views.

FEMINIST Someone who believes men and women should be treated equally.

FUNDAMENTALIST Someone who follows a religion in its strictest form.

GENETICIST Someone who studies how organisms pass on characteristics.

GEOLOGIST Someone who studies Earth's physical structure.

HOLOCAUST The mass murder of Jews and other minority groups by Nazi Germany in concentration camps.

HUMAN RIGHTS Basic rights that belong to everyone on Earth, based on dignity, equality, and fairness.

INDIGENOUS Originating in, or native to, a particular area.

LGBTQ+ Short for Lesbian, Gay, Bisexual, Trans, Queer, and others, meaning all those who don't identify as heterosexual (attracted to members of the opposite sex) and cisgendered (someone whose gender identity matches their sex at birth).

NEUROBIOLOGIST A scientist who studies the brain and nervous system.

PALEONTOLOGIST A scientist who studies fossil evidence of past life.

PERSECUTION Treating someone very badly, usually because of their race, beliefs, or sexual identity.

PHILANTHROPIST Someone who gives generous support to charities.

PHILOSOPHER Someone who studies big questions, such as the nature of knowledge, reality, and existence.

PHYSICIST A scientist who studies matter and energy.

PREJUDICE An unfair opinion that is not based on fact.

PRIMATOLOGIST Someone who studies primates.

PROTEIN A type of molecule that is needed for growth and repair.

PSYCHOLOGIST A scientist who studies the human mind.

RADIATION A form of energy that travels as rays or waves and is invisible to the human eye.

RADIOACTIVE Describes unstable atoms (the smallest units of an element) that release high-energy particles when they break apart.

SEGREGATION Separating people into groups, usually according to their race.

SUFFRAGIST Someone who wants more people—usually more women—to be able to vote.

X-RAY A type of radiation that can pass through many materials.

INDEX